Lowcountry Delights
Cookbook & Travel Guide

Second Edition
2003

A collection of recipes from
favorite Bed and Breakfast Inns, Historic Inns, and Restaurants
in The Lowcountry

Beaufort, South Carolina
Charleston, South Carolina
Savannah, Georgia
St. Simon's Island, Georgia

ஒ-ஒ

Maxine Pinson & Malyssa Pinson

SSD, Inc.
d/b/a
The INNside Scoop
www.innsidescoop.com
The Food Scoop
www.thefoodscoop.com
Savannah Restaurants Online
www.eatinginsavannah.com

Savannah, Georgia

Published by
SSD, Inc.
22 W. Bryan St.-- PMB 202
Savannah, GA 31401

Cover/Layout Design: Maxine Pinson   **Copy Editor:** Malyssa Pinson

Authors' photograph: Jason Chervenak   **Food consultant:** Frank Ciccone

Original Artwork

Amy Moreno (pp. 26, 28, 36, 38, 54, 66, 68, 72, 74, 76, 80, 88, 90, 108, 112,
        116, 126, 130, 136, 138, 140, 142, 146, 150, 152, 155, 156, 158, 162)
www.illustrationsbyamy.com (dearlake@aol.com)

Theron Wallis (pp. 25, 43, 94, 103, 132, 134, 144)

First Printing	*May 2002*	*4,000*
Second Printing	*July 2003*	*3,000*

Library of Congress Control Number: 2003093167

> **An order form for *Lowcountry Delights***
> (including a special "Value-pack")
> **is available on page 221.**
> One may also be printed from: www.thefoodscoop.com/lcd.html

Disclaimer and Limits of Liability

While the authors and publisher have used their best efforts to insure the accuracy of all information at press time; changes do transpire, especially when there is a change of management or ownership. Therefore, SSD, Inc. does not guarantee the accuracy or completeness of any information and is not responsible for any errors or omissions or the results obtained from use of such information. This book is sold as is without any warranty of any kind, either expressed or implied. Neither the authors nor SSD, Inc. or its distributors shall be liable to the purchaser or any other person or entity with respect to any liability, loss, or damage caused or alleged to be caused directly or indirectly by this book.

ISBN 0-9716662-2-9

WIMMER
COOKBOOKS
ConsolidatedGraphics
1-800-548-2537

＊＊＊＊＊＊＊＊＊＊＊＊＊＊＊＊＊＊＊＊＊＊＊＊＊＊＊＊

To Celia,
our much missed daughter and sister

To Billy,
our much loved husband and father

To Sara,
dearly loved mother and grandmother

And to Lois,
our special friend

＊＊＊＊＊＊＊＊＊＊＊＊＊＊＊＊＊＊＊＊＊＊＊＊＊＊＊＊

The Scoop on Lowcountry Delights

The selection of the B&Bs and Historic Inns, included in *Lowcountry Delights,* was based upon the following criteria:

- Hospitality and personal warmth of innkeepers
- Willingness to accommodate the requests of guests, when possible
- Professionalism of innkeepers
- Appearance of interior and exterior of inn
- Furnishings, style/design, room decor
- Attention-to-detail
- Distinctive features
- The quality and presentation of breakfast
- Amenities and conveniences
- Availability and upkeep of grounds or garden area
- Location of inn and consideration of area attractions
- Private baths
- Respect for the privacy of guests
- Telephones in room, preferred but not mandatory
- Value of accommodations and services received
- Historical significance, when applicable
- Honesty and congruency in marketing
  (Web site and brochure *accurately* represent the inn)
- The integration of each of the 5 senses (sight, sound, taste, touch, smell) into a unique inn experience

Authors' notes: *No payment was received for any inclusion in this book. Each inn and restaurant featured, listed, or photographed has been personally experienced by either one or both of the authors; featured inns and restaurants have been visited since 1999. Some of the inns and restaurants are big-time operations, others are family-run and operate on a smaller scale. The inns range from private homes, where the innkeepers live with their family, to urban mansions filled with museum-quality antiques. The restaurants range from a 5-Diamond dining room to one located on the ground level of a 19th century townhouse where guests participate in communal dining. There is an inn and restaurant in this book to suit every taste!*

The selection of the restaurants, included in *Lowcountry Delights*, was based upon the following criteria:

- Selection and uniqueness of menu
- Service and food knowledge by server
- Timely delivery of meal
- Presentation of meal

- Decor and ambience
- Friendliness of staff
- Location
- Value of meal for price paid

The Selection and Testing of Recipes included in *Lowcountry Delights*

The recipes included in this book were either requested, specifically, by the authors or chosen by the contributor in accordance with the authors' guidelines. An attempt was made to select a wide range of Lowcountry cuisine as well as recipes that are quick 'n easy for novice (and "don't-like-to-cook") cooks and challenging recipes for gourmet cooks with advanced culinary skills.

Maxine says, "While editing the recipes, Malyssa (as a beginner cook) made certain each recipe was clear enough so she would feel comfortable preparing it alone. She brought to my attention ingredients and/or terminology needing clarification. It was through the testing of these recipes—alone and with me—that Malyssa learned to cook. She now enjoys cooking more than I do. It has been a fun, learning, and rewarding experience for each of us."

All recipes, included in this cookbook, have been tested in a non-commercial kitchen. They were tested either by one of the authors or a member of *Lowcountry Delights'* testing team (see listing on page 6)—individuals ranging from a ten-year-old to an octogenarian. The majority of the recipes have been double-tested, and a number of the recipes have been triple-tested. Notes or suggestions are included, at the end of many recipes, to assist in easier preparation of the dish or ideas for variations of the recipe. In addition, pronunciation is provided for most of the non-English words and notes of historical interest (about a recipe or an ingredient) are included with selected recipes. Substitutions are included for hard-to-find ingredients or guidance is provided for locating the item.

Why *Lowcountry Delights* is one-of-a-kind cookbook/travel guide

Our research reveals *Lowcountry Delights* is the only cookbook/travel guide available including *all* of the following features:

- No payment for inclusion

- Basic information provided, at a quick glance, about each inn and restaurant

- Favorite local dining establishments recommended in locations of B&Bs/ Historic Inns

- The inclusion of a sketch or photograph of each inn/restaurant featured, enabling one to get a feel for its style and ambience in advance

- A section on dining etiquette addressing basic questions one may have prior to dining out (especially at an upscale restaurant) or having breakfast at a B&B

- A comprehensive Q&A section, for inn-goers (laced with "inntertaining" inn-related anecdotes) familiarizing guests with the B&B concept before making a visit to one

Acknowledgements

Special gratitude is extended to:

Tricia Ainsworth, Frank Ciccone, Rose Ciccone, Patty Croft, Frances Davis, Jan de Voest, Mariette and Claude Gagne, Keith Josefiak, Pamela Lanier, Emily Lineback, Amy Moreno, Jackie Morrison, Lee Morrison, Bill Pinson, Patsy Rach, Jim and Carol Ruddick, Brent Savage, Sandy Soule, Sheila Thomas, Marcia Thompson, Lois Ward, recipe contributors and testers, advisory board members, special friends who believed "we could and we would"—and who provided supportive encouragement from beginning to end. We extend heartfelt thanks to each of you.

Recipe Testers

Eva Avery, GA	Helen Jungmann, GA	Patsy Rach, AL
Ashlee Brady, NC	Sharon & Jim Mahanes, SC	Jennifer & David Price, SC
Jason Chervenak, GA	Anatasia Miltiades, GA	Martha Rowe, VA
Rose & Frank Ciccone, NY	Marsha Moore, GA	Kate Sadler, GA
Amanda & Morgan Colburn, MD	Jackie Morrison, SC	Lynda Salisbury, AL
Marian English, VA	Marge Morken, MS	Debbie Shealy, GA
Mariette Gagne, NC	Judy Nelson, TX	Lyn Springer, SC
Lawson Hardee, SC	Donna Nichols, GA	Genna Wangness, GA
Celia Hilliard, IL	Joanne Pemberton, AL	Vikki Woods, TN
Linda & Mike Johnson, GA	Maxine & Malyssa Pinson, GA	Zeke Zechella, GA

Note: Frank Ciccone, the food consultant for *Lowcountry Delights*, attends the Culinary Institute of America in Hyde Park, NY. In addition to providing willing assistance to us, concerning numerous questions while editing and testing the recipes, he also did a final proofing of the recipe pages (assisted by his wife, Rose, Associate Editor of *BedandBreakfast.com Report*). Thanks to their untiring efforts, the recipes in this book are much easier to follow than they would have been otherwise.

Credit for Photographs & Quotes

Beaufort Chamber of Commerce
for permission to use photograph of Beaufort on back cover

Charleston Area Convention and Visitors Bureau
for quotes on Charleston

Middleton Place
for permission to use photograph of Middleton Oak

Savannah Area Convention and Visitors Bureau
for quotes on Savannah

Lee Morrison
Pages 96 & 163
Photograph of Charleston's bandstand on back cover

The Cover Photograph
(in addition to The Tidal Creek--p. 23, The Lowcountry Oaks--p. 206, and The Napping Cat--p. 166)
taken by Maxine Pinson at Laurel Hill Plantation

Advisory Board
for Innformation Section

David and Wendy Adams
Adams Edgeworth Inn--Monteagle, TN
www.assemblyinn.com

Gale and Jim Chapman
Prestwould Bed & Breakfast--Flat Top, WV
www.prestwould.com

Ruth and Jim Edwards
John Penrose Virden House--Lewes, DE
www.virdenhouse.com

Joe Finnegan
St. Francis Inn--St. Augustine, FL
www.stfrancisinn.com

Peggy and Tom Flint
Folly Castle Inn--Petersburg, VA
www.follycastle.com

Harriet and Jim Gott
Bufflehead Cove Inn--Kennebunkport, ME
www.buffleheadcove.com

Donna and Bob Marriott
Casa Sedona--Sedona, AZ
www.casasedona.com

Jane and Brian McGreevy
Hayne House--Charleston, SC
www.haynehouse.com

Celeste and Harry Neely
The Nicholson House--Athens, GA
www.nicholsonhouseinn.com

Peggy Patteson and Bill Westbrook
The Hope and Glory Inn--Irvington, VA
www.hopeandglory.com

Gloria and Bob Rogers
Four Rooster Inn--Tabor City, NC
www.4roosterinn.com

Donna Sparks
The Granite Steps--Savannah, GA
www.granitesteps.com

Winky and Cecil Staton
Harmony House--Rock Hill, SC
www.harmonyhousebb.com

Anne and Bob Washburn
The Chalet Club--Lake Lure, NC
www.chaletclub.com

Mary and Roger Wolters
Red Horse Inn--Landrum, SC
www.theredhorseinn.com

Vikki Woods
Iron Mountain Inn--Butler, TN
www.ironmountaininn.com

Jackie and Lee Morrison
"Innkeepers Emeritus"
Laurel Hill Plantation Bed & Breakfast
(1986-2001)
McClellanville, SC

Note: *The Advisory Board consists of innkeepers whose inns have been reviewed or recommended by The INNside Scoop bed & breakfast newsletter. These inns par excellence, located in different areas of the country, are recommended with pride and pleasure. Photographs, of each inn, may be seen on pages 202-203. Deep appreciation is expressed, to each of these innkeepers, for their input and feedback on the Q&A section found on pages 168-201.*

About Cover Photograph

Laurel Hill Plantation Bed and Breakfast
(1991 - 2001)

*W*hen the original Laurel Hill Plantation house was constructed in 1850, Richard Tillia Morrison (the current owner's great-great-grandfather) owned more than 20,000 acres in the area. Laurel Hill was a turpentine plantation that produced lumber and naval stores. The Morrison family sold Laurel Hill in the 1950's, and the new owners used the land for truck farming. Except for short periods, when migrant workers stayed in the house, it was vacant.

For over 20 years, Jackie Morrison longed to own the abandoned house and begged the owners to sell it. They finally agreed to sell the house, but not the land. A stipulation was made that the house had to be moved, in its entirety, and the site had to be left in pristine condition.

In January 1983, Jackie and Lee Morrison moved the Laurel Hill Plantation House from Highway 17 to its present location on another part of the original plantation tract. Restoration of the dilapidated house moved slowly, but the results were remarkable. In May of 1985, Laurel Hill was listed on the National Register of Historic Places. A year later, Laurel Hill was featured in *Country Living* magazine. In July 1986, the Morrisons opened their country home as a bed and breakfast inn--a true Lowcountry delight.

On September 21, 1989, Hurricane Hugo hit the South Carolina coast with a twenty foot tidal surge and 200 m.p.h. winds. The house at Laurel Hill was destroyed--nothing was left. The Morrisons refused to give up their dreams and set about designing a replacement house, based on the plan of the lost house.

On July 1, 1991, Laurel Hill Plantation Bed and Breakfast was re-opened in the new structure. The Morrisons operated Laurel Hill as a B&B for fourteen years. During that time, Jackie also served as president of the South Carolina Bed and Breakfast Association (2000-2002). Jackie and Lee retired from innkeeping in January 2002; however, they continue sharing their idyllic Lowcountry home with friends on a regular basis.

A conservation easement on Laurel Hill Plantation has been granted to The Nature Conservancy by the Morrisons.

See pages 160-161 for a collection of Jackie Morrison's
Laurel Hill Plantation's B&B recipes and an order form for Jackie's cookbook.

Introduction

by Pamela Lanier

When Maxine asked me to write the introduction to her cookbook I was thrilled, not only because Maxine is a wonderful supporter of bed and breakfasts, but also because Southern cooking, and especially Lowcountry cooking, is one of my very favorite cuisines. It's only natural, I guess, since I grew up in Tennessee and have spent many happy summers visiting family members on Lowcountry beaches. The whole area from Beaufort, South Carolina, to "the marshes of Glynn" resonate strongly throughout my family due, in part, to my forbear, the poet Sidney Lanier, whose poems so beautifully capture the magic of the area.

Beauty and magic abound in the Lowcountry, and the inns Maxine has chosen are perfect reflections of the area. What is most delightful about this book is that you have the opportunity to bring some of the inns' atmosphere home. Preparing these wonderful dishes in your own kitchen can fill your heart and home with the same warmth and pleasure kindled at the inn's table.

The warmth and pleasure of bed and breakfasts and country inns have fascinated me ever since I returned from a post-college trip to Europe where I stayed in B&Bs and small inns. I was so captivated that I wrote a guidebook entitled *The Complete Guide to Bed & Breakfasts, Inns & Guesthouses.* I've just completed its 19th edition. What is it about these lodgings that I find so compelling? Why am I still enthralled after so many years in the industry?

Well, first of all, like a snowflake each inn is unique, shaped by the building's architecture and décor, the innkeepers' personalities, and the region in which it is located. With no two being alike, I am assured of distinctly different and inspiring experiences at each inn I visit. Secondly, I love being pampered-- and, for me, breakfast in bed or tea served in my room is the ultimate in pampering. Just to lean back into the pillows sipping my tea and nibbling on a freshly baked muffin, perusing a magazine or gazing out a window at the surrounding countryside--to me this is heaven.

And I do not think I am very different from most inngoers. After a hectic week at the office, they arrive at an inn ready for that pampering, enveloping environment and the unique experience that lets them know they are somewhere special, a place where they can shed the week and rejuvenate. Nothing says "change of pace" more for the average working person than to wake up ensconced in a feather bed surrounded by a beautiful, romantic ambience with the smell of coffee wafting upstairs. Here they can savor breakfast, the one meal of the day most busy folks do not have the luxury of enjoying. An assembly-line bagel, scoffed down on the way to an early-morning meeting, can hardly compare to the lavish, relaxing repast spread before them at a country inn.

Which brings me to the third reason I am still passionately involved in this industry--country inn cuisine. Being a great breakfast fan, the thrill of a new breakfast every morning in itself is enough to keep me going! As the cuisine an inn serves is as unique as the inn itself, each meal is a new and exciting celebration of local ingredients and ambience. A successful inn cannot be separated from the region in which it is located, and the most successful inn cuisine reflects this regional character.

Sharing--recipes, stories, family photographs--is what brings guests and innkeepers together. Who can forget conversations around a gorgeous breakfast table amidst heaping platters of fresh fruit, home-baked breads, and fragrant egg dishes? What makes these meals so memorable is sharing joy and laughter with other guests and the innkeepers themselves. At that table, in that special inn, no one is a stranger, ages and occupations are not significant, barriers melt away as easily as warm butter on a stack of flapjacks.

Have I become jaded by bed and breakfasts? Never!

I hope you enjoy the beautiful and delicious recipes from Lowcountry inns--and imagine yourself nestled by the warmth of their hearths.

Bon Appétit!

Pamela Lanier
www.TravelGuides.com

Pamela Lanier is the author of The Complete Guide to Bed & Breakfasts, Inns and Guesthouses (currently in its 19th annual edition), host of the Yahoo! Gold Star recipient web site TravelGuides.com, and editor of four bed and breakfast cookbooks. She also serves as director of Bed & Breakfast Inns and Guesthouses International, with a membership of over 7,000 inns.

Photo courtesy of Middleton Place--Charleston, SC

The Middleton Oak, located upon the magnificent grounds of Middleton Place outside Charleston, served as an Indian Trail tree long before Columbus discovered America. Overlooking the Ashley River, the Middleton Oak's enduring grace and beauty captures the essence of The Lowcountry and the captivating mystique that is uniquely hers.

Foreword

by Maxine Pinson

❧❧❧❧❧❧❧❧❧❧❧❧❧❧❧❧❧❧❧❧❧❧❧❧❧❧❧

Living in The Lowcountry, for the past thirty years, has been a highlight of my life. No matter where I go—in this country or abroad—when I say I am from Savannah, there is almost always instant recognition. Positive comments follow, and I feel proud and privileged to live where I do. The Lowcountry—boasting Beaufort, Charleston, and Savannah—is an uncommon place. The uniqueness of The Lowcountry is no longer a secret.

After publishing a parenting publication in Savannah, for five rewarding years (1990-1994), I expanded it to Beaufort and Charleston, SC. My newsmagazine, *Savannah Parent,* became *Lowcountry Parent*—and I became familiar and enchanted with Beaufort and Charleston. It was during this time that I first began writing travel articles and recommending area restaurants to my readers. It was also when I re-discovered B&Bs. By this time, bed and breakfasts inns had become "discovered" and were popping up throughout The States.

Due to a series of crisis-level personal circumstances, I had to make the painful choice of discontinuing my parenting publication in the fall of 1995. At that point-in-time, I could no longer meet the demands of publishing *Lowcountry Parent* without compromising the high quality and service to which I was committed. To give less than my best was something I was unwilling to consider. However, by then, publishing was in my blood. I knew I would never be able to give it up completely—too many writing ideas were swirling in my head.

Since 1989, I have wanted to pursue a writing career. I knew I would not rest in peace until this desire was fulfilled. The last issue of my parenting publication came out in October 1995; the first issue of *The INNside Scoop*—a Bed and Breakfast newsletter "Dedicated to the Discovery of Bed and Breakfast Getaways"—made its debut in December 1995. I had no concept, at that time, of the joys awaiting me as I moved forward into the next chapter of my life. I continue to be amazed, and I continue to be grateful.

For the first five years, *The INNside Scoop* was a 4-page quarterly newsletter featuring bed and breakfast inns in Georgia and the Carolinas; it then became an 8-page bi-annual newsletter featuring inns in Georgia, the Carolinas, plus four additional states. Beginning with the July 2003 edition, each issue includes reviews of B&Bs in five states (I'm slowing down!) and 12 inns recommended in different parts of the country. Each newsletter also features signature recipes from B&Bs I have visited. A photograph is shown of each inn, and suggestions are made for dining in the town where each inn is located. These recommendations are also online at www.thefoodscooop.com. Each inn and restaurant, appearing in *The INNside Scoop* Bed & Breakfast newsletter, is rated upon criteria I use in determining how highly I feel I can conscientiously recommend it to others. I only recommend inns/restaurants personally experienced by me, and payment is not accepted for a review or a recommendation.

I first became hooked on bed and breakfasts (see page 170) during 1971 when my husband, Bill, and I spent the summer in Europe. Since that time, I have had the opportunity of experiencing hundreds of inns—large, small, and in-between—in all parts of this country.

How It Happened: "The Tracks of Max"

In the spring of 1989, at the lowest and loneliest point in my life, I heard an inspirational message that touched and changed my life forever. However, it was not until much later that I realized what a tremendous impact the content of the message had upon me. It sparked a growing desire within me to spend the rest of my life providing affirmation, encouragement, and hope to others in a way that would be meaningful and lasting.

I have always felt that good can evolve from evil, and this belief has brought me to where I am today. If it had not been for a personal trauma I experienced in 1989 (to be addressed, in detail, in future books), I never would have returned to my college alma mater to take courses in journalism, speech, and technical writing. Little did I know how helpful these courses would prove to be in the years ahead. I only knew that taking them was something I felt inexplicably compelled to do, and I have learned to trust my instincts. Seldom do they mislead me.

A few months after completing my courses, I was contacted by a publisher in Atlanta requesting that I become editor for a new parenting publication, *Savannah Parent*. He had met me through my daughter, Celia, who was a staff writer for a teen newspaper published by him. I was totally intimidated by the idea of editing a newspaper, and so I refused—adamantly. However, a few weeks after my second refusal, 20,000 copies of the new publication were shipped to Savannah. I was listed as editor, even though I had absolutely nothing to do with that edition. After overcoming my initial annoyance, I began feeling cajoled that someone had that degree of confidence in me and my potential. Holding my breath, I accepted editorship of *Savannah Parent*. The decision was one I never regretted.

After 3 months, during which time I was working 60-plus-hour weeks, I was still waiting on my first paycheck as editor of *Savannah Parent*. Finally, two checks arrived on the same day. Each bounced. Long story made short: after sending a couple of letters to the publisher and consulting with an attorney, I did some bouncing—right into the position of owner, publisher/editor/ad representative/marketing director for *Savannah Parent* newsmagazine.

I am not known to be a silent sitter; just not my modus operandi. I discovered early in life, especially as a woman reared in the Deep South, that being "nice and sweet" does *not* always produce positive results. When one is taught (directly or indirectly) to suppress thoughts and feelings, rather than feeling free to express them without fear of retribution, a destructive cycle spirals into motion. The pattern continues until it is recognized and broken. Mustering the courage to stand up and confront an unacceptable situation can have unpleasant consequences, but it can also be liberating and self-affirming. These are issues I plan to address in a future book, possibly a novel, based upon my life's story and those of other women I know.

People often ask how I "got started" with *The INNside Scoop*. Now you have it—the inside scoop on *The INNside Scoop! Savannah Parent* is the grandparent of *The INNside Scoop*, which is the parent of *Lowcountry Delights*. It is my hope that an inspirational writing ministry, launched with *52 Scrolls* (see page 211), will be the next offspring of this sequel.

The INNside Scoop
is a bi-annual Bed and Breakfast newsletter
published each January and July.
It is available online at:

www.innsidescoop.com

A complimentary e-subscription to the newsletter is

nlsub@cs.com

In 1998, at the end of what I refer to as my "decade of hell," Bill and I lost our first child, Sara Cecilia, to a rare and vicious form of cancer (mycosis fungoides). We shall always be grateful for the time God entrusted our beautiful daughter to us, a child doctors once told me I was incapable of conceiving. I appealed to the Great Physician, and my prayers for a child were finally answered. God sent us Celia, but only for a short time. Our daughter was only 23-years-old when she died, so young and full of promise. Yet, the legacy she left continues to inspire individuals who knew her as well as those who never met her (see www.innsidescoop.com/Celia.htm). Her inimitable spirit will live forever.

When Celia died, I felt a big part of me died with her. I survived, emotionally, by staying busy. And, yes, I confess: my busyness tends to be obsessive, but it channels my restless energy into productivity and keeps me afloat. Five months after losing Celia, remembering the message of hope I had heard at another low point in my life, I applied and was accepted (as an extended campus student) at Union Theological Seminary-Presbyterian College of Christian Education in Richmond, Virginia. Union-PSCE is a theological institution of the Presbyterian Church (USA). No, I am not preparing to become a pastor. I am attending seminary preparing for a writing ministry through which I want to recycle the hope, encouragement, and inspiration I have received from countless others.

If we should ever meet, and I hope we will, don't you worry about having to deal with some proof-texting religious fanatic. I am very outspoken about the pushing or forcing of one's religion or personal ideology upon another person. Try doing it with me, and you'll never suspect I'm a seminarian! It is because of my intolerance of religiosity (based upon my "experience of '89"—see www.innsidescoop.com/SpiritualAbuse.htm) that I became interested in attending seminary. I wanted to learn more about my faith, but I did *not* want it shoved down my throat through cultic machinations or an indoctrination process (www.innsidescoop.com/UnhealthyReligion.htm).

Today some of my dearest and most cherished friends are innkeepers. I consider them a special "breed." As much as I love staying in their incomparable bed and breakfasts and historic inns, what I cherish most are the relationships formed as a result of a snoop named Max trying to get the facts--the *innside scoop* on their bed and breakfast or historic inn. I hope you know, my friends, how much I care about and appreciate you.

Jackie and Lee Morrison, whom I have taken the liberty of proclaiming as "innkeepers emeritus," know about hope and the encouragement it provides. The story of how they acquired their inn (cover photo), only to have it decimated by Hurricane Hugo, may be read on page 8. On the first page of a cookbook Jackie compiled, she pens: *Laurel Hill Plantation: 1850. Carried to sea by Hurricane Hugo—September 21, 1989; Rebuilt 1990-91.*

The Morrisons were devastated by their loss, as anyone would be. But Jackie and Lee did not permit their unfortunate circumstances to wash away their lives or zest for living. Instead, they rebuilt and started anew. The house they rebuilt is even better and stronger than the original structure. Perhaps our common "steel magnolia" resolve is why Jackie and I became close friends in such a short period of time. Neither of us is afraid of "telling it like it is."

Life has taken me on many journeys during these past years, and not all paths have led to pampering bed and breakfast inns. During my years as a travel writer/restaurant reviewer, I have enjoyed fine dining at its best. I have also gleaned "food for thought"—lessons in life allowing me to see human beings, from varied backgrounds, and material stuff through clearer lenses. However, of all the memorable trips I have taken, my most meaningful journey has been an inner one that has forever forged my faith and made me acutely aware of my personal dependence upon God for daily guidance and perseverance in all that I do.

It is my hope that *Lowcountry Delights* will guide you to delightful and memory-making journeys, introduce you to delectable new dishes, and maybe even provide a little "food for thought" en route to whatever your final destination in life may be. May each of your sojourns leave you with a reservoir of delightful and lasting memories, and may all the calories consumed evaporate as you travel to your next adventure!

--*Maxine Pinson*
May 2003

Table of Contents

ৡ৾

Beaufort, SC

B&Bs and Historic Inns

Restaurants

Charleston, SC

B&Bs and Historic Inns

Restaurants

Charleston Area
B&Bs and Historic Inns

Restaurants

Savannah, GA
B&Bs and Historic Inns

Restaurants

(continued on next page)

Tybee Island, GA

B&B

Restaurant

St. Simon's Island, GA

B&B

Restaurant

Other Recipes

INNformation for INNgoers

Our Story

Other

Recipes

from

The Lowcountry's
Most Delightful Inns & Restaurants

*Good food and gracious hospitality
flow through The Lowcountry like a tidal creek*

"It's a place where fresh water meets salt and where creeks, marshes, and rivers meld with sunshine, tides, and sea breezes."
---*Southern Living* (April 2003)

≫-≫-≫-≫-≫-≫-≫-≫-≫-≫-≫-≫-≫-≫-≫-≫-≫-≫

Beaufort lands a coveted spot on the *2001 National Trust for Historic Preservation* list of "12 Distinctive Destinations"-- travel treasures providing "striking alternatives to Anyplace, USA."

≫-≫-≫-≫-≫-≫-≫-≫-≫-≫-≫-≫-≫-≫-≫-≫-≫-≫

USA Today names Beaufort, SC as "one of 10 great places to honeymoon---or renew nuptial bliss---for romantics seeking an All-American destination." The article refers to Beaufort as a "sleeper hit, a sweet coastal gem filled with sweet B&Bs and the sweeping verandas of antebellum mansions."
--- *USA Today* (October 22, 2001)

≫-≫-≫-≫-≫-≫-≫-≫-≫-≫-≫-≫-≫-≫-≫-≫-≫-≫

Beaufort is one of 50 towns chosen for inclusion in the 2001 edition of *The 50 Best Small Southern Towns*. The guidebook selects small southern towns portraying a "gentler way of life." According to the authors: "Beaufort exudes charm. The many historic homes, built in the late 1800's and early 1900's, gracefully enhance the town's color-ful character. Live oak trees, draped with Spanish moss, grace the brick walkways and narrow streets; the town commands spectacular water views in three directions. No wonder several movies have been filmed in Beaufort."

--- Gerald Sweitzer and Kathy Fields

Web Site for Beaufort, SC
(pronounced "Bew-fort")

www.beaufortsc.org

Beaufort
"Beauty by the Bay"

Original artwork by Theron Wallis

Typical scene in the enchanting moss-draped,
history-filled community of beautiful Beaufort, SC

The Beaufort Inn

Located in the center of Beaufort's Historic Landmark District,
The Beaufort Inn offers an impeccable sense of style
where great expectations are quietly met.

Address: 809 Port Republic Street
Beaufort, SC 29902
(Historic District)
Telephone: (843) 521-9000
E–mail: bftinn@hargray.com

Web Site: www.beaufortinn.com
Category: Historic Inn
Owner: Associated Luxury Inns of Beaufort
Rates: $135-$235 (year-round)

Citrus-Scented Banana French Toast

5-6 ripe bananas, sliced
16 crusty slices of French bread
10 eggs
4 cups milk
3 tablespoons sugar
Grated rind of 2 oranges

1 tablespoon cinnamon
½ teaspoon allspice
¼ teaspoon cardamom
1 tablespoon vanilla extract
Butter for frying

Place banana slices between bread slices to make 8 banana sandwiches. Mix eggs and next 7 ingredients in a wide, shallow dish; whisk until smooth. Dip sandwiches into batter until thoroughly soaked. Fry sandwiches in butter until golden. Transfer to a buttered cookie sheet to keep warm.

Yield: 8 servings

❧❧❧❧❧❧❧❧❧❧❧❧❧❧❧❧❧❧❧❧❧

Poppy Seed Waffles

1½ cups all-purpose flour	3 large eggs
6 tablespoons sugar	1¼ cups buttermilk
3 tablespoons poppy seeds	¼ cup (½ stick) unsalted butter, melted
1½ teaspoons baking powder	2 teaspoons vanilla
¼ teaspoon salt	

In large bowl, mix first 5 ingredients until combined. In a small bowl, whisk eggs and add next 3 ingredients to blend. Add buttermilk mixture, all at once, to flour mixture and whisk until just blended. Let mixture sit 15 minutes. Preheat waffle iron according to manufacturer's instructions. Spoon batter onto waffle iron; cover and cook until golden and cooked through-out, about 7 minutes (cooking time varies, depending on waffle iron). Repeat with remaining batter. Serve immediately with warm Papaya Orange Chutney.

Yield: 6 servings (using approximately ¾ cup of batter per pancake)

Papaya Orange Chutney

4 papayas, peeled, seeded, and thinly sliced	1 cup orange marmalade
½ cup orange juice	½ teaspoon Chinese five-spice powder

Combine all ingredients in a medium saucepan. Simmer, stirring occasionally, until papaya is tender and mixture slightly thickens, about 10 minutes.

Editors' Notes: *Chinese five-spice powder can be found in the Oriental section of upscale grocery stores and in most Asian food markets. To serve this dish, we suggest dusting the waffles with powdered sugar and spooning the Chutney directly onto center of waffle. Garnish with a sprig of fresh mint.*

"One of the Top Ten Most Romantic Inns in The USA"
-- *The Road Best Traveled*, 1998

Named one of the "Top Ten Inns in the Country"
by American Historic Inns.

"From check-in to check-out,
the Beaufort Inn is a haven of wonderful experiences."
-- Karen Lingo, *Southern Living Magazine*

Craven Street Inn

*This lovely Victorian home, built as a private residence in 1870,
creates a new standard for casual, affordable elegance.*

Address: 1103 Craven Street
Beaufort, SC 29902
(Historic District)
Reservations: 1-888-522-0250
Telephone: (843) 522-1668
E-mail: cravenstinn@hargray.com

Web Site: www.thecravenstreetinn.com
Category: B&B
Owner: Associated Luxury Inns
of Beaufort
Innkeeper: Geoff Nimmich
Rates: $125-$225 (year-round)

Spinach and Leek Quiche

1½-2 tablespoons olive oil or butter
1 medium leek (white and green parts),
trimmed and chopped
½ small onion
4 eggs
1 cup heavy cream
½ teaspoon salt

¼ teaspoon freshly ground pepper
A generous pinch of nutmeg
Dash of red pepper flakes
1 (6-ounce) bag fresh spinach,
coarsely chopped
4 ounces sharp Cheddar cheese, grated
1 pre-baked pie crust

Preheat oven to 375°. In sauté pan, sauté leek and onion in oil or butter. In a large bowl, whisk eggs with cream and next 4 ingredients. When the leek and onions are translucent (not brown), add spinach and cook until just wilted. Add leek and spinach to egg mixture. Place the grated Cheddar into pie shell and cover with egg and spinach mixture. Bake until quiche (KEESH) is puffed and golden (about 30 to 40 minutes).

Yield: 6 servings

Editors' Note: *Frozen onions and spinach may be substituted for fresh vegetables.*

Pear Coffee Cake
Topping

½ cup butter
½ cup flour
1 cup brown sugar

4 teaspoons cinnamon
2 cups pecans or walnuts,
  finely chopped

Using a fork or pastry blender, cut together first three ingredients. Mix in cinnamon and nuts.

Cake

½ cup butter
¾ cup sugar
2 teaspoons vanilla
2 fresh eggs
2 cups all–purpose flour
1 teaspoon baking powder

1 teaspoon baking soda
½ teaspoon salt
1 cup sour cream
2½ cups pears--approximately
  4-5 Bosc pears (peeled, cored,
  diced)

Cream butter and sugar until light; add vanilla and eggs. In a separate bowl, mix together next 4 ingredients. Add flour mixture to butter mixture, alternately, with sour cream. Fold in pears. Spread cake batter into a greased and floured 13 x 9-inch pan. Cover with topping. Bake at 350° 40 minutes. Cut into squares.

Yield: 16 servings

Editors' Notes: *The Bosc pear, available October through April, has a sweet-tart flavor. After pouring cake batter into pan, fill any empty spaces with extra nuts before baking.*

Built as a single family residence in 1870, the house served as the residence of the Lipton family for almost 75 years. Mr. Lipton was the cobbler at Parris Island who made all the boots for the Marine Corps recruits.

The Rhett House Inn

*A place full of history, romance, and relaxation
providing the simple pleasures of an authentic plantation house.*

Address: 1009 Craven Street
Beaufort, SC 29902
(Historic District)
Reservations: 1-888-480-9530
Telephone: (843) 524-9030
E-mail: info@rhetthouseinn.com

Web Site: www.rhetthouseinn.com
Category: Historic Inn
Owners/Innkeepers:
Steve & Marianne Harrison
Rates: $150-$350 (seasonal)

Southern Grits

1 cup coarse, stone-ground grits
4 cups water
2-4 tablespoons chicken-base paste

2-4 tablespoons butter
Milk or half-and-half, as needed

Combine all ingredients. Cook over low heat for about an hour, stirring occasionally. Cover and put into refrigerator overnight. The next morning, resume cooking. Add milk/half-and-half until desired consistency is reached or as needed. Cook over low heat for about an hour.

Yield: 6-8 servings

Editors' Notes: *Stone-ground grits and chicken-base paste are available at gourmet and specialty food stores. No substitute for either of these ingredients is recommended. Use less chicken-base paste for a less salty taste and more if you prefer a saltier taste; 3 tablespoons was just the right amount for us. We also prefer using half-and-half (about 2 cup) instead of milk. The result is creamier and richer. We did not find it necessary to continue cooking grits an additional hour the next morning. They just need warming up. These grits are definitely more time-consuming than instant grits, but they are about the best grits we G.R.I.T.S. ("Girls raised in the South") have ever tasted.*

Bed & Breakfasts and Historic Inns
Beaufort, South Carolina

Cheese Hot Bites

1 cup flour	¼ teaspoon salt
2 cups Cheddar cheese, shredded	½ teaspoon cayenne pepper
½ cup butter	1 cup pecans, chopped

Cream all ingredients, except pecans, together by hand. Stir in pecans until well mixed; roll into logs. Wrap logs in wax paper and chill in refrigerator overnight. Thinly slice and bake on an ungreased baking sheet 10 to 15 minutes in a 325° oven; do not brown. Sprinkle salt on wafers while still warm. Logs may be frozen.

Yield: 4 logs

Editors' Notes: *Before baking, sprinkle with sesame seeds and paprika. Store in an airtight container.*

Pecan Pie
Filling

1¼ cups dark brown sugar	4 eggs
¾ cup light corn syrup	2 cups pecans
¼ cup melted butter	2 teaspoons vanilla

Blend all ingredients. Pour into 9 or 10-inch pie dish lined with unbaked pie shell. Bake at 400 degrees for 10 minutes. Finish baking at 325° for 30 minutes or until set. Cool.

Crust

¾ cup shortening	2 cups flour
1 cup boiling water	1 teaspoon salt
1 tablespoons milk	

Whip shortening into boiling water until fluffy; whip in milk. Add remaining ingredients, blending until moist. Form into a ball and roll out onto a floured surface. Place into a pie pan. and prick bottom with a fork.

Yield: 6 servings

Editors' Note: *For 12 individual tarts, half pie filling recipe. After rolling out dough for crust, use a biscuit cutter to cut out 3-inch circles. Place dough in a muffin tin and spoon in filling. Bake same as for pie. Serve pie or tarts with vanilla ice-cream or cool whip.*

> "One of the best inns in The South."
> -- Southern Living

Two Suns Inn

By far the best view in Beaufort

Address: 1705 Bay Street
Beaufort, SC 29902
(Historic District)
Reservations: 1-800-532-4244
Telephone: (843) 522-1122
E-mail: info@twosunsinn.com

Web Site: www.twosunsinn.com
Category: B&B
Owners/Innkeepers:
Henri & Patricia Safran
Rates: $130-$168 (seasonal)

Filled Shaken Omelet

4 large eggs
Salt and pepper, to taste
4 teaspoons water
2 teaspoons butter

1 cup finely cut smoked salmon
1 tablespoon sour cream, to taste
Chopped fresh dill to garnish

Break eggs in small bowl; season with salt and pepper. Add water and beat no more than 30 strokes or until minimal amount of foam develops. Melt butter in an 8-inch non-stick skillet (hold skillet at a 45 degree angle to burner). Rapidly shake pan back-and-forth so egg mixture is thrown against the pan's sides; using a spatula helps with distribution of eggs. Return pan to burner. Rotate pan so any uncooked egg in center moves to perimeter of pan. Cook evenly 20 to 40 seconds. Quickly place salmon and sour cream in center of omelet. Fold omelet over filling by tilting pan a little higher off the burner and using a spatula to fold it over. Turn omelet onto a plate. Sprinkle with dill and serve.

Yield: 2 servings

Editors' Note: *The key to success is speed and heat. Smoked ham (sliced and cubed) or another meat may be substituted, if desired, for the salmon. Chopped chives provide a good alternate garnish for this dish.*

Prune Clafouti

½ cup sugar
1½ cups pitted prunes
3 eggs
1 tablespoon vanilla extract

¼ cup all purpose flour
1 cup milk
1 cup heavy cream

Preheat oven to 375°. Butter a quiche pan (approximately 2 inches deep) or a 2 quart casserole dish. Sprinkle 2 tablespoons of sugar over bottom of cooking container; scatter prunes (or other fruit) on top. In a blender, combine eggs, vanilla, and remaining sugar; blend until smooth. Add flour and blend briefly. Add remaining ingredients and blend until all ingredients are incorporated. Pour mixture over fruit and bake about 45 minutes or until puffed and browned. Set aside to cool for 15 minutes before serving. Serve warm.

Yield: 6 servings

Editors' Notes: *Another fruit (pitted cherries, plums, nectarines, peaches, pears, blueberries, or strawberries), may be substituted for the in the clafouti (kla-foo-TEE) for the prunes.. A wonderful way to begin breakfast, especially during the cooler months.*

Mini Apple Tarte Tatin

1 cup sugar
¼ cup water
4 tablespoons unsalted butter
½ cup fresh cranberries, chopped

½ cup walnut halves, chopped
12 Lady Apples, peeled and cored
   from the bottom, stems intact
1 sheet frozen puff pastry, defrosted

Preheat oven to 400°. Whisk sugar together with ¼ cup water. Without stirring, cook mixture over medium heat until amber-colored (320° to 350° on a candy thermometer). Pour 1 tablespoon of the caramel into the bottom of each cup of a 12-cup muffin pan. Add 1 teaspoon of butter to each cup and set aside. Combine cranberries and walnuts; fill each apple with mixture. Place apples, stem side down, into caramel. Roll out puff pastry to a 12-inch square. Cut out 12 (2½-inch) circles and place over apples, tucking pastry around apples. Bake until golden brown and puffed, 30 to 35 minutes. Invert immediately, onto a serving plate, and serve (stem side up with pastry on bottom) while warm.

Yield: 12 servings

Editors' Notes: *Lady Apples have a sweet-tart flesh and are brilliant red to yellow (with red blushing) in color. If Lady Apples are unavailable for the tarte Tatin (tart tah-TAN), Fuji or Braeburn apples may be used instead. Use dried cranberries if fresh ones are not in season.*

> "Perched atop the highest spot in historic Beaufort,
> the bayview from Two Suns mesmerizes the onlooker."
> --*The INNside Scoop*, June 1996

The Beaufort Inn

Offering three exceptional dining experiences

Address: 809 Port Republic Street
Beaufort, SC 29902
(Historic District)
Telephone: (843) 521-9000

Web Site: www.beaufortinn.com
Cuisine: Contemporary Southern
Executive Chef: Keith Josefiak
Price Range: Dinner/$16-$29

Beaufort Inn She Crab Soup

¼ pound unsalted butter
½ small yellow onion, diced
½ tablespoon fresh garlic, chopped
½ cup flour
1 bay leaf
½ teaspoon fresh thyme, chopped
¼ teaspoon nutmeg
½ tablespoon Worcestershire sauce
½ cup dry sherry

2 cups whole milk
1 cup heavy cream
½ cup crab stock, clam juice,
   or 2 tablespoons commercial crab base
½ pound crab (blue, preferred) claw meat,
   picked clean of shell
⅛ cup crab roe, cleaned
Salt and fresh black pepper, to taste

Melt butter in a heavy-bottomed stockpot; sauté the onion and garlic for 5 minutes until softened. Stir in flour and whisk until smooth, creating a roux which will thicken the soup. Cook for 5 minutes. Add remaining ingredients, except for crab and roe; whisk thoroughly to remove all lumps. Bring to a boil and stir until thickened. Season to taste, using lots of black pepper and salt. After puréing crab and roe in a food processor, gently stir it into the soup mixture. Adjust consistency, if needed, by adding more milk.

Yield: 4-5 servings

Editors' Notes: *Crab stock is sometimes available already prepared in specialty shops, where crab base may also be found. These items may also be ordered from online gourmet shops such as www.superiortouch.com or www.gatewaygourmet.com. Fresh crab roe is only available in the spring.*

❧❧❧❧❧❧❧❧❧❧❧❧❧❧❧❧❧❧❧❧❧❧❧❧❧❧❧❧

Shrimp and Grits

1 pound large shrimp, peeled and deveined
¼ cup olive oil
1 tablespoon garlic, chopped
½ cup smoked tasso ham, diced fine
½ cup sun-dried tomatoes
  (soaked, drained, and minced)
½ cup dry white wine

2 cups heavy cream
2 tablespoons butter
Salt and pepper, to taste
1 cup grits, cooked
  (according to directions)
Parmesan cheese

In a very hot sauté pan, sear shrimp in olive oil; stir constantly. Add next 3 ingredients and continue stirring. Deglaze with wine and add cream. Cook an additional 2 to 3 minutes. Remove shrimp to a serving dish; cover to keep warm. Continue cooking sauce until thickened. Add butter and adjust seasoning. Pour sauce over shrimp and serve over cooked grits flavored with Parmesan cheese.

Yield: 2 servings

Editors' Note: *Tasso ham can usually be found at upscale grocery stores or delicatessens. However, Italian cappacola, prosciutto, or slices from a country ham may be substituted.*

Molasses Pecan Butter

1 pound unsalted butter, room temperature
½ cup toasted pecans, finely ground
½ cup maple syrup

⅛ cup molasses
½ tablespoon salt

Cream butter in mixer, add remaining ingredients. Blend well. Roll into tubes of wax paper and freeze. Use as needed.

Yield: 1¼ pounds

Editors' Note: *This delicious butter, wonderful on biscuits, molds beautifully!*

"Top Inn Dining" -- *Country Inns Magazine*

"A *must* dining experience"-- *The Atlanta Constitution*

"Four Stars Outstanding" -- *Savannah News* restaurant review

Featured on "Dining Around" -- The Television Food Network

Featured on "Great Chefs of the South"
    -- Public Broadcasting Television Network

Bistro 205

Fine dining in a relaxed setting

Address: 205 West Street
Beaufort, SC 29902
(Historic District)
Telephone: (843) 524-4994

Web site: www.bistro205.com
Cuisine: American Continental
Executive Chef/Proprietor: Gary Lang
Price Range: Dinner/$17-$26

Ginger-Dusted Ahi Tuna with Asian Peanut Sauce

2 (6-ounce) yellowfin tuna filets, sushi grade
2 tablespoons ground ginger
Salt to taste

Ground black pepper
Sesame seeds
4 tablespoons canola oil

Dust the tuna filets with ginger; lightly cover with salt and pepper. Sprinkle each side with sesame seeds and set aside until ready to cook.

Sauce for Tuna

1 cup soy sauce
3 tablespoons mirin wine
1 cup orange juice

1 tablespoon minced ginger
1 tablespoon creamy peanut butter

Mix all sauce ingredients in a bowl and whisk well. Add mixture to a sauté pan and heat until liquid starts to thicken. Be careful not to reduce too much as sauce will become overpowering. Heat oil in a pan over high heat; add tuna when pan is just about to smoke. Sear each side until crust is formed. Be careful to maintain a nice, rare center. Pour sauce over tuna to serve.

Yield: 2 servings

Editors' Notes: *Ahi (AH-hee) is the Hawaiian name for yellowfin tuna. Mirin wine (also referred to as rice wine) is a basic ingredient in Japanese cooking and can be found in Asian markets or the gourmet section of some supermarkets.*

Filet Mignon
with Potatoes Napoleon and Apple Bacon Spinach

16 ounces beef tenderloin steak, trim fat
Salt and pepper, to taste
1 baking potato, cut into "waffle" chips
1 purple potato, cut into "waffle" chips
4 ounces Stilton cheese

⅛ apple, finely diced
2 tablespoons butter
2 slices bacon
12 ounces fresh spinach leaves

Salt and pepper tenderloin. Grill to desired doneness. Cut potatoes into "waffle" chips with a mandoline and place on a sheet pan. Weight potatoes down with another sheet pan on top. Bake in a 350° oven for 30 minutes or until just brown. Layer potatoes with alternating layers of Stilton cheese. Bake for an additional ten minutes. Melt butter in a frying pan and sauté apple until softened. Meanwhile, cook bacon. Drain and dice. When apple is soft, add bacon to pan. After apple-bacon mixture is hot, add spinach leaves and cook until wilted. Season with salt and pepper. Layer one-half of the potatoes, all of the spinach, and the remaining potatoes. Top with grilled filet tenderloin.

Yield: 2 servings

Editors' Notes: *A mandoline is a small kitchen aid with various adjustable blades for slicing firm fruits and vegetables into varied shapes. Fresh potatoes may be substituted with frozen cottage fries (thaw before using). Stilton is the English version of blue cheese.*

"Locals will steer you toward the upscale dining at Bistro 205.
It's quite satisfying!" -- *Southern Living,* April 2003

Magnolia Bakery Cafe

A refreshing neighborhood eatery with patio dining under the magnolias

Address: 703 Congress Street
Beaufort, SC 29902
(Historic District)
Telephone: (843) 524-1961

Web site: www.thefoodscoop.com/mbc.html
Cuisine: Contemporary American
Executive Chef: Dana Johnsrude
Price Range: Lunch only/$3.95-$7.25

Creamy Cucumber Soup

4 large cucumbers
¼ cup unsalted butter
1 medium onion, diced
¼ teaspoon salt (optional)
¼ cup flour
1 bay leaf
¼ teaspoon ground white pepper

½ teaspoon dill weed (double if using fresh)
2 tablespoons chopped parsley
6 cups chicken stock
1¼ tablespoons fresh lemon juice
1 teaspoon grated lemon rind
1 cup sour cream
Milk to lighten soup (optional)

Peel cucumbers and slice in half lengthwise. Scoop out seeds with a Parisian scoop or teaspoon and slice about 1-inch thick. Melt butter and soften onions over medium-high heat in a 3 to 6 quart stockpot. Add cucumbers and salt; cook for 5 more minutes. Stir in flour and cook for 2 minutes. Add seasonings, chicken stock, lemon juice, and rind. Simmer for 30 minutes and chill in the refrigerator or over an ice bath. Purée the soup with the sour cream. Milk should be stirred in to lighten the soup, if desired. Serve chilled and garnish with fresh dill.

Yield: 4-6 servings

Editors' Notes: *Canned chicken broth may be substituted for chicken stock. Serve with fresh tomato sandwiches for a tasty summer lunch.*

ട്ര<del>ട്ര</del>ട്ര<del>ട്ര</del>ട്ര<del>ട്ര</del>ട്ര<del>ട്ര</del>ട്ര<del>ട്ര</del>ട്ര<del>ട്ര</del>ട്ര<del>ട്ര</del>ട്ര<del>ട്ര</del>

Baked Ham and Cheese Strata

5 large eggs
2½ cups whole milk
½ teaspoon onion powder
¼ teaspoon ground black pepper
½ teaspoon salt

5 ounces fresh bread crumbs
 (cut into ½-inch cubes)
5 ounces Cheddar cheese, shredded
6 ounces baked Virginia ham,
 finely chopped (use a food processor)
2 ounces Cheddar cheese, shredded

Beat together eggs and milk; stir in next 3 ingredients. Spray or butter sides and bottom of a 1 quart soufflé or casserole dish. Spread bread crumbs evenly in bottom of dish. Sprinkle 5 ounces of cheese over the bread and pour in liquid mixture. Refrigerate overnight. Top with ham and bake in a 350° oven 45 to 55 minutes. The strata should be golden brown with a puffy appearance. Top with remaining 2 ounces of cheese and let rest 10 minutes before serving.

Yield: 4-6 servings

Editors' Note: *Use your imagination to create different variations of this delicious strata.*

Magnolia Bakery Cafe's Lemon Squares

1 cup unsalted butter (2 sticks)
¼ cup powdered sugar
1⅛ cups all-purpose flour
4 large eggs
2 cups granulated sugar

2½ tablespoons all-purpose flour
1 teaspoon baking powder
2 tablespoons lemon rind,
 fresh or dried
½ cup fresh lemon juice (2 lemons)

To make the crust: beat together first 3 ingredients in a large mixing bowl until fluffy. Scrape mixture into a greased 6" x 8½" sheet pan, patting into place with dampened fingers. Bake in a preheated 325° oven for 15 minutes. In a medium bowl, beat together eggs and sugar. Using a whisk, blend in remaining 4 ingredients and pour into the crust. Bake at 325 degrees for 30 to 40 minutes or until the filling is set. Cool before cutting and garnish with powdered sugar.

Yield: 12-15 large Lemon Squares

Recommended as a "Favorite Spot" for lunch in Beaufort
by TheFoodScoop.com

Plum's Waterfront Cafe

Casual dining on the waterfront

Address: 904½ Bay Street
Beaufort, SC 29902
(Historic District)
Telephone: (843)525-1946

Cuisine: Eclectic American
Executive Chef: Joshua J. McLean
Price Range: Lunch/$5-$10
Dinner/$13-$22

Plum's Turkey Apricot Nut Salad

2 cups chopped, smoked turkey breast
¼ cup golden raisins
¼ cup dried apricots, roughly chopped
¼ cup toasted almonds (chopped)

½ cup medium onion, diced
½ cup Hellmann's mayonnaise
Salt and pepper to taste
Lettuce

Combine all ingredients, chill, and serve over lettuce.

Yield: 4-6 servings

Editors' Note: *We also enjoyed a variation of this salad substituting scallions for regular onions and slivered, toasted almonds for chopped almonds. This is a refreshing luncheon dish and attractive served atop curly green lettuce garnished with sliced apricots.*

ﬗﬗﬗﬗﬗﬗﬗﬗﬗﬗﬗﬗﬗﬗﬗﬗﬗﬗﬗﬗﬗﬗﬗ

Grilled Filet with Brandied Chèvre

1 medium onion, thinly sliced	Small can of artichoke hearts
8 fresh garlic cloves	Salt and pepper, to taste
Olive oil	2 (8-ounce) filet mignons

Oil a sauté pan and bring to medium-high heat. Add sliced onion and sauté, cooking and stirring until the onion begins turning a golden brown. Allow onion to attain a dark brown color to fully release its natural sugars into the pan. Continue cooking until caramelization is reached. Submerge garlic cloves in olive oil and cook in a 450° oven until tender. Squeeze excess water out of artichoke hearts by taking handfuls and squeezing each handful individually. Lay the hearts onto a sheet pan and season with salt and pepper. Bake at 250° until artichokes become crispy and golden around the edges.

Brandy Blue Chèvre Sauce

1 cup heavy cream	¼ cup Maytag blue cheese
¼ cup brandy	¼ cup chèvre (goat cheese)

Add all ingredients together in a sauce pan and bring to medium heat, stirring constantly. When sauce begins to thicken, it is ready. Adjust the taste with salt, if needed.

Season filets (fih-LAYS) with salt and pepper. Grill over charcoal, wood, or a stove-top grill. Top each filet with caramelized onions, artichoke hearts, and garlic. Top with the chèvre (SHEHV) sauce.

Yield: 2 servings

Chosen as Beaufort's "Best All-Round Restaurant"
by *Lowcountry Weekly* (1999 & 2000)

"A crowded little place with a waterfront deck that seems to do almost everything well." --*Washington Post (*10-22-00)

"The bustling Plum's Cafe boasts 'creative casual cuisine and a prime waterfront location'." --*Atlanta Constitution Journal* (5-9-01)

For the ninth consecutive year, readers of *Condé Nast Traveler* name Charleston as "One of the Top 10 Travel Destinations in North America." (2001)

&·&·&·&·&·&·&·&·&·&·&·&·&·&·&·&·&·&

The Charleston, SC area receives distinction
in the October 2001 issue of *National Geographic Traveler*,
as one of the "Top 50 Places of a Lifetime: America."

&·&·&·&·&·&·&·&·&·&·&·&·&·&·&·&·&·&

Bride's Magazine honors the Charleston area as a "Top U.S. Destination"
in its 2001 Worldwide Honeymoon Guide

&·&·&·&·&·&·&·&·&·&·&·&·&·&·&·&·&·&

"Charleston will turn the head of the most arrogant modernist. The brick-paved street lined with cast-iron lamps, the rows of pastel-colored houses-all conspire to make the city one huge antique: British colonial with a warm Southern breeze."
—*Conde Nast Traveler*

&·&·&·&·&·&·&·&·&·&·&·&·&·&·&·&·&·&

Charleston claims the top spot for the eighth consecutive year
on Marjabelle Young Stewart's "Most Mannerly" list. (2000)

&·&·&·&·&·&·&·&·&·&·&·&·&·&·&·&·&·&

'Suddenly, a warm fresh breeze turns up our collars and causes the swags of moss to sway gracefully, like billowing curtains. There is something in the air. It is not the familiar tang of the sea or the perfume of Confederate jasmine, nor is it the pealing of church bells or the delicate rustle of palmetto fronds. It is romance."
—Stephanie Fletcher for *The Buffalo News*

&·&·&·&·&·&·&·&·&·&·&·&·&·&·&·&·&·&

"Everything living has to change with the times, and I, for one, am as glad Charleston is a living city as I am that it remembers the past. As long as it can hold on to both, it will always be a place we want to go."
—Mel White for *National Geographic Traveler*

Web Site for Charleston, SC
www.charlestoncvb.com

Charleston
"Champion of Character and Charm"

Original artwork by Theron Wallis

The Battery captures the charismatic charm of Charleston

1837 Bed & Breakfast Tea Room

Featuring open piazzas, rockers, and Southern hospitality

Address: 126 Wentworth St.
Charleston, SC 29401
(Historic District)
Reservations: 1-877-723-1837
Telephone: (843) 723-7166

Web Site: www.1837bb.com
Category: B&B
Owners/Innkeepers: Sherri Weaver
Richard Dunn
Rates: $79-$175 (seasonal)

Eggnog Bread

1 cup eggnog
¼ cup brandy
¾ cup canola oil

2 teaspoons melted butter
3 eggs
1 box yellow cake mix

Preheat oven to 350°. Mix first five ingredients together. Add cake mix. Using hand mixer, blend all ingredients. Pour mixture into a Bundt pan sprayed with Pam. Bake for 30 to 35 minutes until golden brown (cake should bounce back when lightly touched). Cool in pan for 15 minutes after removing from oven. Turn out of pan and place on a pedestal cake plate. Do not cover until completely cooled to room temperature. This is a very moist cake and becomes soggy if covered too soon.

Glaze

2 cups powdered sugar   2-3 tablespoons eggnog

Mix ingredients together; mixture will be thick and appear unspreadable. Glaze cake when it is almost cooled. The warmth from the cake will help the glaze slide down the sides of the cake.

Yield: 1 cake

Editors' Notes: *Do not use a cake mix with pudding in it or the cake will be too wet. If eggnog is unavailable at the supermarket, eggnog (such as Mr. Boston creamy eggnog) can be purchased at a liquor store and works just as well. A perfect breakfast bread (or cake to serve with coffee) for the holidays. It freezes well.*

Sausage Balls

1¾ cups Bisquick   ½ pound Jimmy Dean sausage, uncooked
5 ounces Cheddar cheese

Mix all ingredients together with hands, breaking up sausage as much as possible. Knead until ingredients are all incorporated and mixture is smooth. Roll into balls and place on a cookie sheet. Bake at 350° for 10 to 15 minutes. Balls should be lightly brown. Be careful not to let bottoms burn. Cool to room temperature.

Yield: Approximately 3 dozen

Editors' Notes: *These sausage balls may be frozen up to 2 months. Defrost and reheat on a baking sheet at 200° for 20 minutes (or reheat in a microwave.*

Cinnamon Swirl Buns
Syrup Mixture

1 stick margarine or butter   2 tablespoons dark corn syrup   1 cup brown sugar

Combine all ingredients in sauce pan. Bring to a boil over medium heat and then reduce heat.

Filling

1 tablespoon butter, melted   1 cup orange marmalade
⅓ cup brown sugar   1 cup pecans, chopped & toasted
2 tablespoons cinnamon   ½ cup raisins, optional
1 cup oatmeal

Mix together all ingredients. Spray cups of muffin pan with Pam. Cover bottom of each muffin cup with toasted pecans. Spoon about 1 tablespoon of syrup mixture over pecans. Set aside.

Buns

1 (10-pack) can of refrigerator buttermilk biscuits

Preheat oven to 350°. Place biscuits, consisting of 5 rows down and 2 across, on counter top (see diagram below). Biscuits should slightly overlap. Pinch seams together so perforations are sealed. Roll out dough so it is even and forms a rectangle. Spread filling over dough and sprinkle with raisins, if desired. Roll dough into a log. Using a sharp knife, cut roll into pieces approximately 1-inch thick. Place each piece into a muffin cup over pecans and syrup mixture. Place muffin pan on top of a sheet pan to catch any overflow of liquid. Bake for 30 minutes. After removing buns from oven, run a knife around each muffin cup to loosen bun. Turn pan upside down onto a sheet of aluminum foil placed on counter top. Let cool.

Yield: 10 buns

"...a perfect place to unwind."
-- New York Times

Ashley Inn

A true taste of The South set in a charming architectural treasure

Address: 201 Ashley Avenue
Charleston SC 29403
(Historic District)
Reservations: 1-800-581-6658
Telephone: (843) 723-1848

E-mail: ashleyinnbb@aol.com
Web Site: www.charleston-sc-inns.com
Category: Historic Inn
Owner/Innkeeper: Barry Caroll
Rates: $89-$250 (seasonal)

Tut's Toffee

35 saltine crackers
2 sticks butter, softened
1 cup brown sugar

1 (12-ounce) package
semi-sweet chocolate chips
1½ cups pecans, chopped

Preheat oven to 350°. Line a (10 x 15-inch) jelly-roll pan or a shallow baking dish with waxed or parchment paper. Place saltines (7 down and 5 across) in pan. Combine next 2 ingredients in a microwave-safe bowl. Microwave on high 2 to 3 minutes; stir thoroughly and pour mixture over crackers. Bake at 350° for 20 minutes. Remove from oven and cover with chocolate chips. Smooth with spatula and sprinkle with nuts. Chill and break into bite size bits.

Yield: 4 dozen pieces

Editors' Note: *Easy and delicious! Store in airtight container. We've served this recipe at many of our book signings, and everyone loves it.*

❧❧❧❧❧❧❧❧❧❧❧❧❧❧❧❧❧❧❧❧❧❧❧❧

Peaches 'n Cream Stuffed Waffles

Peaches

2 fresh peaches, peeled and thinly sliced—save some for garnish

Waffle Batter

2 cups waffle mix
¾ cup milk
¾ cup water

2 eggs
1 teaspoons vanilla
1 teaspoon orange extract

Mix ingredients together and prepare waffles on a preheated waffle iron.

Filling

6 ounces cream cheese, softened
½ teaspoon orange extract

¼ cup powdered sugar

Whip all ingredients together with an electric mixer. Spread 1½ tablespoons filling on one-half of waffle. Top with peach slices and fold over. Keep warm.

Praline Sauce

1 cup brown sugar
½ stick butter
¼ cup water (or maple syrup)

½ cup whole pecans
¼ cup sour cream
Sprigs of mint, optional

Combine first 2 ingredients and melt in a saucepan. Add next 2 ingredients. Top stuffed waffles with Praline Sauce. Garnish with a dollop of sour cream, more peach slices, and a sprig of mint.

Yield: 4 servings

Editors' Note: *If time is short, use frozen waffles.*

"Charleston's Gourmet Breakfast Place"

Recipient of prestigious "1997 Carolopolis Award"

Featured in the nationally televised
"Country Inn Cooking with Gail Greco" on PBS.

━━━━━━━━━━━━━━━━━━━━

*Built in 1832 by Alexander Black,
an inventor of rice and cotton processing equipment*

Cannonboro Bed & Breakfast

A place to be pampered with very special southern hospitality

Address: 184 Ashley Ave.
Charleston, SC 29403
(Historic District)
Reservations: 1-800-235-8039
Telephone: (843) 723-8572

E-mail: cannonboroinn@aol.com
Web Site: www.charleston-sc-inns.com
Category: Historic Inn
Owner/Innkeeper: Barry Caroll
Rates: $89-$250 (seasonal)

Sausage Turnovers

Cheese Sauce

1½ cups white sauce (any recipe)
½ cup Cheddar cheese, shredded
¼ Parmesan cheese, grated

⅛ teaspoon oregano
Pinch of cayenne pepper

Make sauce using your favorite basic white sauce recipe, a white sauce mix (prepared as directed), or a prepared white sauce. Stir in remaining ingredients. Keep warm.

Turnovers

1 pound sausage
½ red pepper, chopped
½ green pepper, chopped
½ onion, chopped

Frozen puff pastry sheets
¾ cup Cheddar cheese, shredded
1 egg

Cook first 4 ingredients together and drain. Thaw pastry sheets and cut into individual squares. Put ¼ cup of sausage mixture in center of each square and top with 2 tablespoons of cheese; fold over, making a triangle. Crimp edges of turnover and press together with prongs of a fork. Brush with egg wash (1 egg whisked with a drop of water and a pinch of salt) and prick holes in top of turnover with a fork. Bake at 425 degrees 15 to 18 minutes. Top with cheese sauce.

Yield: 4-6 servings

Editors' Note: *Instead of pricking top of turnover with a fork, a simple design (see example at right) can be "carved" into top of pastry with tip of a knife.*

Bacon and Tomato Dip

½ pound bacon
8 ounces sour cream

8 ounces cream cheese, softened
½ large tomato, chopped

Cook bacon (in frying pan or microwave) until crisp; drain. Mix together next 2 ingredients (adjusting amount of sour cream, if desired). Stir in bacon, tomatoes, and desired seasonings. Chill until ready to use and serve with crackers.

Yield: Approximately 1½ cups

Editors' Note: *Also makes a nice spread on an open-faced tea sandwich.*

Kit Kat Bars

1½ cups graham cracker crumbs
¾ cup brown sugar
1 cup granulated sugar
¾ cup butter
⅓ cup milk

Butter crackers (such as Waverly)
1 cup butterscotch chips
1 cup semi-sweet chocolate chips
¾ cup peanut butter

Put first 5 ingredients into a saucepan and bring it to a boil. Boil for 5 minutes, being careful not to burn. Set aside. Place a layer of crackers in a greased 9 X 13-inch pyrex dish and cover with one-half of sugar mixture. Top with another layer of crackers and cover with remaining mixture. Add a third layer of crackers on top. Make topping by melting last 3 ingredients together in a saucepan over low heat. Spread mixture over top layer of crackers and let cool. Cut into squares.

Yield: 24-30 squares

A Charleston single house, built in the Victorian style, the home was built in 1853 by a wealthy rice planter. The house is particularly noted for its two circular piazzas featuring twenty-two massive columns.

Fantasia Bed & Breakfast

A classic Charleston single-house in Charleston's historic district

Address: 11 George Street
Charleston SC 29401
(Historic District)
Telephone: (843) 853-0201
Reservations: 1-800-852-4466

E-mail: reservations@fantasiabb.com
Web Site: www.fantasiabb.com
Category: B&B
Owners/Innkeepers: Marty & Cathy Riccio
Rates: $95-$205 (seasonal)

Marty's Italian Tomato-Basil Frittata

½ small Vidalia onion, thinly sliced
½ fresh tomato (ripe and juicy), diced
4 large eggs
2 tablespoons half-and-half

⅛ cup grated Romano cheese
2-3 leaves of fresh basil
Salt and pepper, to taste

Sauté sliced onion in skillet until soft and tender. Dice tomato and cook with onions for two minutes. Combine remaining ingredients; add tomato and onion to egg mixture. Return mixture to skillet and cook until eggs begin taking shape, be careful not to over-brown bottom. Remove skillet from top of stove and place under broiler to finish the frittata. The frittata is done when eggs are lightly colored and set.

Yield: 4-5 servings

Editors' Note: *Chopped peppers (green and/or red) add variety and color to this excellent frittata (frih-TAH-tuh).*

Fantasia's Spicy Pecans

2 egg whites, slightly beaten
2 teaspoons water
2 (16-ounce) bags shelled pecans
1½ teaspoons salt
½ cup sugar

1 tablespoon cinnamon
¼ teaspoon nutmeg
¼ teaspoon allspice
¼ teaspoon ginger

Preheat oven to 300°. Combine egg whites and water. Add nuts and toss to coat. Combine next 6 ingredients. Add to nuts and toss until coated. Place in single layer on lightly greased baking sheet. Bake for 20 to 25 minutes.

Yield: 15-20 servings

Editors' Note: *Put in a holiday tin for a special gift during the holidays.*

Orange Sherbert Delights

½ cup butter
1 cup sugar
2 eggs
¼ teaspoon vanilla extract
½ teaspoon orange extract

1 tablespoon milk
2½ cups flour
¼ teaspoon salt
2 teaspoons baking powder
2 tablespoons sugar

Preheat oven to 375°. Cream butter; add 1 cup sugar and blend. Add eggs, one at a time, and next 3 ingredients. Combine next 3 ingredients and add to butter mixture. Beat until well-blended. Place 2 tablespoons sugar in a bowl. Take rounded teaspoons of batter (or a melon scooper), roll in sugar, and place on a lightly greased cookie sheet. Bake 15-20 minutes.

Yield: 3 dozen medium cookies

Editors' Note: *Instead of using vanilla and orange extracts, use 1 tablespoon lemon extract to convert these tasty cookies to Lemon Sherbert Delights. Each flavor is good sprinkled with granulated sugar after baking.*

Known as the Mary Scott House, this single-house dwelling stands on land Miss Scott inherited in 1791 from her grandfather, Daniel Legare, one of Charleston's earliest developers.

Governor's House

*One of the most elegant and historically significant homes in Charleston,
a city whose past is part of its soul.*

Address: 117 Broad Street
Charleston, SC 29401
(Historic District)
Reservations: 1-800-720-9812
Telephone: (843) 720-2070
E-mail: governorshouse@aol.com

Web Site: www.governorshouse.com
Category: Historic Inn
Owners/Innkeepers: Karen Spell Shaw
Robert Hill Shaw, III
Rates: $165-$330 (seasonal)

Baked Grapefruit

Brown sugar
1 red grapefruit (ripe, but firm)
Honey *or* sherry, 1 tablespoon per grapefruit half

Preheat oven to 350 degrees. Cut grapefruit in half and section with a grapefruit knife. Brush tops of grapefruit with honey or sherry. If brushed with sherry, sprinkle with brown sugar. Bake for 15 to 20 minutes until warm.

Yield: 2 servings

Editors' Note: *A wonderful first-course breakfast dish during the fall and winter months. Garnish with a maraschino cherry or an edible flower.*

Bed & Breakfasts and Historic Inns
Charleston, South Carolina

Haystacks

1 (12-ounce) bag of Nestle's white chocolate chips
1 cup of pretzel sticks, broken into small pieces
1 cup Spanish peanuts
Dried cranberries, about a handful

Melt white chocolate chips in a double-boiler. Stir in remaining ingredients and mix well. Drop small spoonfuls of the mixture onto wax paper. Cool.

Yield: Approximately 3 dozen pieces

Editors' Notes: *Cranberries are wonderful for fall treats, but they may be substitued with another fruit or omitted. White chocolate chips may be melted in a microwave, but be careful not to overheat.*

"Check into Charleston's Governor's House Inn
and you may never want to check out."
--Karen Lingo, *Southern Living* (September 1999)

Over 200 years ago, during Charleston's Golden Age, this magnificent home was the residence of Governor Edward Rutledge, the youngest signer of the Declaration of Independence. Here, he and his wife, Henrietta Middleton, received some of the country's most prominent leaders.

Hayne House B&B

An oasis of character and charm near The Battery

Address: 30 King Street
         Charleston, SC 29401
         (Historic District)
Telephone: (843) 577-2633
E-mail: haynehouse@yahoo.com

Web Site: www.haynehouse.com
Category: B&B
Owners/Innkeepers: Brian & Jane McGreevy
Rates: $135-$285 (seasonal)

Robie's Sausage and Egg Casserole

¼ pound bulk sausage (mild or spicy)
¾ tablespoon butter
⅛ cup chopped mushrooms
¼ cup cream or half-and-half

4 eggs
¼ cup New York sharp Cheddar
     cheese, grated

Brown sausage in skillet; crumble and drain. Spread sausage in bottom of a casserole dish. Sauté mushrooms in butter; drain and mix with cream in a separate dish. Soft scramble eggs and layer on top of sausage. Spread mushroom/cream mixture over eggs. Sprinkle grated cheese over top. Cook at 350° for 20 minutes or until cheese is melted and casserole is bubbly.

Yield: 4 servings

Editors' Note: *An egg substitute product may be used instead of fresh eggs. Garnish with fresh basil.*

ๆๆๆๆๆๆๆๆๆๆๆๆๆๆๆๆๆๆๆๆๆๆๆๆๆๆๆๆๆๆๆๆๆๆๆๆๆๆ

Mrs. Lacey's Pound Cake

3 sticks Country Morning Blend
  butter (or margarine)
3 cups sugar
6 eggs

3 cups cake flour
1 (8-ounce) carton sour cream
1 teaspoon vanilla

Do not preheat oven. Thoroughly grease and flour Bundt pan. Cream butter and sugar together. Add eggs one at a time, beating well after each. Alternately, add flour and sour cream. Add vanilla. Place pan in oven. Turn oven on and bake at 325° for 1½ hours.

Yield: 1 pound cake

Editors' Notes: *For variety, other flavorings (i.e., almond, lemon, orange, rum) may be substituted for the vanilla. Very good served at breakfast with fruit.*

Hayne House Pumpkin Bread

4 eggs
2½-3 cups sugar
  (depending on personal taste)
1 cup oil
1 cup cold water
1 (15-ounce) can pumpkin

2 teaspoons pumpkin pie spice
1 teaspoon salt
1 teaspoon cinnamon
2 teaspoons baking soda
1 teaspoon baking powder
3⅓ cups all-purpose flour

Beat eggs and stir in next 4 ingredients. Sift together dry ingredients and add to pumpkin mixture. Mix well. Divide into 2 large or 3 medium-sized loaf pans. Bake at 350 degrees for 60 to 75 minutes until done.

Yield: 2 or 3 loaves

Editors' Notes: *Muffins offer another variation of this recipe (lessen the cooking time) and delicious served chilled with cream cheese. This popular recipe can also be baked in a jar for a unique gift presentation. Pour mixture into a greased wide-mouth pint jar and fill half-full. Place filled jars on cookie sheet and bake at 325° for 45 minutes. When done, remove one jar at a time and wipe sealing edge with a paper towel. Screw cap on tightly, and the heat will vacuum-seal jar. Bread will keep up to one year in sealed jar.*

Selected as one of the top three inns in Charleston
and the only one with a top-rated breakfast.
-- *Travel Holiday* (February 2002)

"This converted Georgian-style single house--true native architecture--
on the residential (read: "Old Money") part of King Street
is pure Charleston." -- Sherri Eisenberg, *Travel Holiday* February 2002

John Rutledge House

America's most historic inn

Address: 116 Broad Street
Charleston, SC 29401
(Historic District)
Telephone: (843) 723-7999
Reservations: 1-800-476-9741

Web Site: www.charminginns.com/
rutledgehouse.html
Category: Historic Inn
Innkeeper: Kathy Leslie
Rates: $165-$375 (seasonal)

Rutledge Biscuit with Hot Sherried Fruit

Sherried Fruit

1 (8-ounce) can pineapple, juice reserved
1 (8-ounce) can of peaches, cut into chunks, juice reserved
1 (8-ounce) can of pears, cut into chunks, juice reserved

¼ cup light brown sugar, firmly packed
⅛ teaspoon ground cinnamon
¼ cup cream sherry (or to taste)
1 teaspoon cornstarch
2 tablespoons water

In a 2 quart saucepan, combine first 3 ingredients and their juices. Add next 2 ingredients and heat through. Stir in cream sherry. In a small bowl or cup, mix corn starch and water. Stir mixture into hot fruit. Cook, stirring occasionally, until thickened.

Biscuits

1 cup self rising flour
⅛ teaspoon baking soda

3 tablespoons shortening
¼ cup buttermilk

In a large bowl, combine first 2 ingredients. Cut shortening into flour with a pastry blender. Add buttermilk and mix just until combined. Turn out onto a floured surface. Knead about 5 minutes or until dough is no longer sticky. Pat or roll to about a ¾-inch thickness and cut with a biscuit cutter. Place on a hot greased baking pan, with sides of biscuits touching. Bake on an ungreased baking pan in a 450° oven until lightly browned (8 to 10 minutes). Serve with hot Sherried Fruit.

Yield: 4 biscuits with fruit.

❧❧❧❧❧❧❧❧❧❧❧❧❧❧❧❧❧❧❧❧❧❧❧

Curried Chicken Salad with Fruit

1 cup chopped or shredded chicken
2-3 teaspoons curry powder
½ cup cream cheese, softened
½ cup mayonnaise

1 large tablespoon Ranch Peppercorn dressing
1 teaspoon sugar
Grapes (purple, green, or both), chopped or whole

Combine and chill first two ingredients. Combine and chill next three ingredients. Combine sugar with remaining ingredients (see note below for suggested additions). Serve with crackers or pita bread.

Yield: 4 servings

Editors' Notes: *Mandarin oranges, chopped pecans, chopped dates, chopped celery, golden raisins, toasted coconut, and/or pineapple bits make a nice addition to this salad. Pineapple-flavored cream cheese provides still another variation. Add more mayonnaise if too dry.*

Rutledge House Inn's Fudge

1 stick (4-ounce) butter
½ stick (2-ounce) margarine
1 small (5-ounce) can evaporated milk
3 cups sugar

1 (12-ounce) bag semi-sweet chocolate chips
½ teaspoon vanilla
1 jar (8-ounce) marshmallow cream

In a 2-quart, heavy sauce pan, heat first 4 ingredients to 234° on a candy thermometer. Add chocolate chips. Allow to soften, then stir in vanilla and marshmallow cream until glossy. Pour into buttered 9 x 13-inch pan. After cool, cut into squares.

Yield: approximately 3 dozen squares

Editors' Note: *This is absolutely the best fudge we have ever sampled! For a mocha-flavored fudge, add 1 teaspoon of instant coffee when sugar is added.*

"Charleston's Classiest Inn"
--Andrew Harper's Hideaway Report (1996)

Named "Top-rated place to stay in Charleston" by
--Conde' Nast Traveler (1999)

John Rutledge, one of the fifty-five signers of the U.S. Constitution, built his home in 1763. Now an exquisitely restored inn, it is the only home of one of these signers which now accommodates overnight guests.

Lowndes Grove Plantation

Overlooking The Ashley River, Lowndes Grove Plantation
proffers 18th century living at its finest

Address: 266 St. Margaret Street
Charleston, SC 29403
Telephone: (843) 723-8438
E-mail: info@lowndesgrove.com

Web Site: www.lowndesgrove.com
Category: B&B
Owners/Innkeepers: Lex & Tina Opoulos
Rates: $125-$165 (year-round)

Muesli with Fruit

2 cups mixed seasonal fruit (assorted berries,
   bananas, apples, pineapples, orange
   sections, pears, nectarines, etc.)
2 cups vanilla low-fat yogurt

1 cup muesli
2 teaspoons honey
2 tablespoons slivered almonds
   or cashews, toasted

Wash and cut mixed fruit into bite-sized pieces. Sprinkle with sugar (or sweetener) to taste. Place prepared fruit in a large cereal bowl, add yogurt, and top with the muesli. Drizzle with honey; sprinkle with almonds or cashews.

Yield: 3-4 servings

Editors' Note: *Muesli ((MYOOS-lee) is a cereal found in most food and health food stores; if desired, granola may be substituted for muesli. Raspberries and blueberries make a tasty and colorful fruit combination. When serving this dish for breakfast, place yogurt and fruit mixture into individual bowls and refrigerate the night before. The next morning, you will just need to top mixture with muesli (or granola), drizzle with honey, and sprinkle with almonds.*

Bed & Breakfasts and Historic Inns
Charleston, South Carolina

ও৺

Peanut Butter and Banana French Toast

3 eggs, beaten
¼ cup cool water
½ teaspoon vanilla extract
2 teaspoons peanut butter
4 slices egg bread (challah)

1 tablespoon margarine
2 bananas, peeled and sliced
   into ½-inch chunks (reserve
   some for garnish)
2 tablespoons real maple syrup

In a shallow bowl, beat water and vanilla into eggs until well-mixed. Spread a teaspoon of peanut butter onto two slices of bread and dip into egg mixture. Then take the other two slices and dip them into egg mixture. Heat margarine in a large frying pan over medium-high heat. When margarine starts bubbling, add the peanut butter slices into the skillet with peanut butter side up. Quickly place banana pieces onto the peanut butter and top with a slice of egg-dipped bread. Squish the sandwich together with a spatula. Let cook about 3 minutes on first side; flip and cook for another few minutes on other side. After 6 or 7 minutes of cooking, if sandwich seems too moist, cover pan with a lid and let cook an additional minute or two. Turn out French toast sandwiches onto big plates and garnish with extra banana slices. Serve with maple syrup.

Yield: 2 servings

Editors' notes: *Challah (KHAH-lah), a traditional Jewish yeast bread, has a light texture and is rich with eggs. For a delicious, crunchy variation, roll sandwich in Corn Flakes before browning.*

> "Offers closest thing you will find to experiencing what life must have been like for the spoiled planter class that ruled the antebellum South.
> — Steve Bailey, *The Boston Globe* (1999)
>
> Lowndes Grove Plantation was selected in 2001 as the setting for a photo-shoot by Tiffany and Company, headquartered in New York City, to convey the lifestyle of Tiffany's clientele.
>
> ___
>
> *The only surviving plantation on the historic Charleston penisula, Lowndes Grove Plantation is listed in the National Register of Historic Places and known as one of "Charleston's 62 most famous homes."*

Two Meeting Street

Charleston's oldest and most renowned inn

Address: 2 Meeting Street
Charleston, SC 29401
(Historic District)
Telephone: (843) 723-7322

Web Site: www.twomeetingstreet.com
Category: Historic Inn
Owners/Innkeepers: Jean & Pete Spell
Rates: $165-$310

Baked Pears with Mango Chutney

9 pears
2 sticks butter
1 (8-ounce) jar mango chutney

1 cup raisins
1 teaspoon cinnamon

Cut pears in half and core. Mix remaining ingredients in a bowl. Stuff 1 teaspoon of butter mixture into each pear. Bake at 350° for 20 minutes. Serve warm.

Yield: 9 pears

Editors' Note: *This mixture may also be used for stuffing apples (leave whole and core). Fruit used may be microwaved until tender and then baked in oven; baste with liquid. Serve stuffed fruit with dairy topping for a tasty dessert.*

Bed & Breakfasts and Historic Inns
Charleston, South Carolina

Ambrosia

4 oranges, sectioned
3 pink grapefruits, sectioned
1 small can chunk pineapple

1 (4-ounce) jar red cherries, drained
½ cup coconut, shredded
½ cup pecans, chopped

Mix all ingredients together, chill, and serve.

Yield: 4-6 servings

Editors' Note: *Add green cherries, along with the red ones, for a festive look at Christmas time. Good served with pound cake (see page 55).*

Cucumber Spread

1 medium cucumber
  (peeled, seeded, and grated)
½ teaspoon garlic power

1 (8-ounce) package of cream cheese,
  softened
1 stick butter

Combine all ingredients. Place in a small glass bowl and serve with crackers or assorted vegetables.

Yield: 1-1½ cups

"Best in the South"
-- *Southern Living* magazine poll
(1999 & 2000)

Featured in *Southern Accents, Southern Living, Travel and Leisure, Country Living, Harper's Hideaway Report, Country Inns and Gourmet,* and served as host for The Discovery Channel's "Great Country Inns of America" series.

The beautiful Queen Anne mansion, given as a wedding gift and completed in in1892, has welcomed guests from all over the world for over 65 years.

Wentworth Mansion

To step through its doors is to step into a world of refinement

Address: 149 Wentworth Street
Charleston, SC 29401
(Historic District)
Reservations: 1-888-466-1886
Telephone: (843) 853-1886

Web Site: www.wentworthmansion.com
Category: Historic Inn
Innkeeper: Bob Seidler
Rates: $315-$695

Cheese Sticks

1¼ cups all-purpose flour
1 teaspoon baking powder
1 teaspoon salt
¾ teaspoon gumbo filé
¼ teaspoon black pepper
¾ teaspoon cayenne pepper

¾ teaspoon granulated garlic
½ cup unsalted butter,
   (cut into small pieces)
1¼ cups white Cheddar cheese,
   shredded
¼ cup grated Parmesan cheese

Mix first seven ingredients together. Whip butter and cheese together; add flour mixture, incorporating it until dough forms a ball. Wrap in plastic wrap and chill 30 minutes or up to 2 days. Preheat oven to 325°. Roll dough into a rectangle (approximately ⅛ inch thick) on a lightly floured surface. Cut dough into strips and transfer them to an ungreased baking sheet spaced 1½ inches apart. Bake for 12 to 16 minutes or until golden brown. After cheese sticks cool, serve immediately.

Yield: 10 servings

Editors' Note: *Gumbo filé ((FEE-lay), made from the leaves of a sassafras tree, is used in Creole cooking and can be found in the spice section of most supermarkets. Top cheese sticks with toasted sesame seeds and sprinkle with paprika. Dough may be frozen and used later.*

Bed & Breakfasts and Historic Inns
Charleston, South Carolina

❧❧❧❧❧❧❧❧❧❧❧❧❧❧❧❧❧❧❧❧❧❧❧❧

Sticky Buns

Buns

1½ ounces yeast	Pinch of salt	5 cups bread flour
1 cup water	1 ounce of Carnation	½ cup cake flour
4 ounces butter	non-fat dry milk	½ cup sugar
½ cup sugar	3 eggs	2 tablespoons cinnamon

All ingredients should be room temperature. Place yeast in a small amount of the water using a separate container. In a mixer, combine next 4 ingredients until well-creamed. Add eggs, one at a time, until incorporated; add water and mix briefly. Add flour and then yeast mixture to the bowl; mix until smooth. Cover dough with plastic wrap and allow to rise for 1½ hours. Preheat oven to 375°. Scale dough into equal parts. On a floured work surface, roll each piece of dough into a 9 x 12-inch rectangle about ¼ inch thick. Brush off any excess flour. Next, brush surface of dough with softened butter and sprinkle with a mixture of sugar and cinnamon. Roll dough up into a 12-inch long log. Cut log roll into 1-inch circular rolls and place on a greased pan with the honey pan glaze and pecan pieces smeared onto the bottom of it. Bake for 12 to 15 minutes or until golden brown. Allow buns to cool before inverting them onto a plate to be served. If they are not completely cool, the glaze will run when inverted.

Honey Pan Glaze

10 ounces brown sugar	2½ ounces corn syrup
4 ounces butter	1 ounce water
2½ ounces honey	

Cream together first four ingredients in a mixer. Add enough water to bring mixture to a spreadable consistency.

Yield: 12 buns

Editors' Note: *This excellent glaze can also be used when baking a ham or to make glazed pecans.*

"Hideaway of the Year" -- *Andrew Harper's Hideaway Report* (December 1999)

One of the "50 Best Secrets" -- *Travel Holiday's* Insider Awards (September 1999)

"Inn of the Month" -- *Travel & Leisure* (November 1998)

Built in 1886 and designed in the Second Empire style as an opulent private residence by a wealthy cotton merchant, the Wentworth Mansion is now one of the world's finest and most unique inns--a pristine example of America's Gilded Age.

82 Queen

Eleven dining areas and a picturesque garden courtyard

Address: 82 Queen Street
Charleston, SC 29414
(Historic District)
Telephone: 1-800-849-0082
(843) 723-7591
Web Site: www.82queen.com

Cuisine: Authentic Lowcountry cuisine
Proprietor: Chef Stephen G. Kish
Price Range: Lunch/$8-$13
Dinner/$16-$22
Cookbook: *The Best of Lowcountry Cuisine*

Grilled Portabello Mushrooms

2 cups oil
2 sprigs rosemary
1 teaspoon salt
1 teaspoon black pepper
1 teaspoon garlic

4-6 portabello mushrooms
(5" diameter with stems removed)
Chèvre (goat's cheese)
Gourmet greens

Mix first 5 ingredients (for marinade) in a shallow pie pan. Place mushrooms in pan and cover with marinade; marinate for 1 to 2 hours or overnight. Mushrooms will absorb most of the marinade. Grill mushroom 5 to 8 minutes per side, cook until tender. Remove, slice, and top with vinaigrette. Garnish with chèvre (SHEHV-ruh) and serve on a bed of gourmet greens.

Yield: 4-6 servings

Vinaigrette

3 teaspoons balsamic vinegar
1 teaspoon olive oil
1 teaspoon brown sugar

1 dash salt
1 dash pepper

Editors' Note: *A savory side dish for grilled steak or pork.*

McClellanville Crab Cakes

1 pound lump crabmeat, picked
½ cup mayonnaise
2 green onions, chopped fine
2 dashes of Tabasco sauce

1 dash of Worcestershire sauce
½ cup coarse bread crumbs
½ ounce fresh lemon juice
½ teaspoon ground thyme

Combine ingredients thoroughly. Form into desired cake size (about 4 ounces each).

Egg Wash

2 eggs   ¼ cup of half-and-half

Make egg wash by combining eggs with half-and-half. Dip crab cakes into egg mixture, then roll into more bread crumbs. Sauté cakes in butter or olive oil until golden brown. Serve with Roasted Red Pepper Cream Sauce.

Roasted Red Pepper Cream Sauce

4 ounces margarine
4 ounces flour
2 cups milk
2 cups fish stock
¼ cup sherry

2 red bell peppers (seeded, peeled, roasted, puréed)
¼ teaspoon cayenne pepper
Salt and white pepper to taste
1 teaspoon paprika
¼ cup bacon fat

In a saucepan, melt margarine over low heat. Add flour and whisk until a roux is formed. Add next 3 ingredients and bring to a boil. Reduce heat and simmer. Add peppers and remaining ingredients. Simmer 10 minutes; strain through a strainer. Add more milk, if too thick.

Yield: 6 servings

Editors' Note: *Crab cakes are a Lowcountry favorite, and these are superb.*

"Reigning in Charleston today--as it has for over fifteen years--is a place renowned in the culinary world for its simplicity and complexity; its grace and casual air; its hearty tables, napery, crystal and decor, coupled with a presentation of food, wine and service so divine as to be, itself, a work of Southern Fiction." *--Hospitality Today*, 1998

"Readers' Choice Awards – Best City Restaurant"
-- Southern Living (1997, 1998, 1999)

Blossom Cafe

A high-energy, contemporary space that perfectly complements the cuisine

Address: 185 E. Bay Street
Charleston, SC 29401
(Historic District)
Telephone: (843) 722-9200 x 1
Web Site: www.magnolias-blossom-
cypress.com

Cuisine: Lowcountry cuisine with
an Italian flair
Executive Chef: Donald Barickman
Price Range: Lunch/$9-$13
Dinner/$16-$27

Pan-Seared Mahi with Tomato-Basil Couscous

Caper Butter Sauce

1 tablespoon lemon juice
1 shallot, diced
1 tablespoon capers, chopped

¼ cup heavy cream
8 ounces butter, room temperature
Salt and pepper

Place first 3 ingredients in a small sauce pan over medium-low heat. Allow mixture to reduce until liquid is almost gone. Next, add cream and reduce mixture until thick. Lower heat and add butter (cut in ½-inch cubes); whisk constantly. Season with salt and pepper. The sauce may be made an hour or two before serving, but hold it at room temperature. Do not reheat as sauce will separate and become unusable.

Couscous

2 cups strong vegetable stock
(chicken stock may be substituted)
½ cup couscous

2 tablespoons diced tomato
2 tablespoons fresh basil
Salt and pepper, to taste

Bring the stock to a boil in a medium saucepan. Add remaining ingredients and stir; remove from heat and allow to sit for 3 to 5 minutes. Fluff with a fork. Set aside, but keep warm.

Mahi Mahi

Olive oil (about 2 tablespoons)
½ cup all-purpose flour

Salt and pepper
2 (6-ounce portions) mahi mahi

Cover bottom of a heavy, oven-proof frying pan with olive oil. Season flour with salt and pepper. Lightly dust fish in seasoned flour and sauté in olive oil until golden brown (make sure fish are not touching as they cook). After turning the fish, place pan in a 350° oven for 5 minutes. Serve fish over couscous (KOOS-koos) and cover with Caper Butter Sauce. Yield: 4

Editors' Note: *Tilapia or cod may be substituted for mahi mahi (MAH-hee MAH-hee).*

❦❦❦❦❦❦❦❦❦❦❦❦❦❦❦❦❦❦❦❦❦❦

Scallopini of Veal with Marsala Wine Sauce

1½-2 pounds veal top round or pounded scallopini   ½ cup flour
   (3 pieces per person, 1¾ ounces per piece)   Olive oil blend, as needed
Salt and pepper, as needed

Slice veal into 1¾ ounce pieces; cover with plastic and pound with a mallet to tenderize and flatten. Do not pulverize (over-pound with mallet). Season veal with salt and pepper. Dredge in flour, shaking off excess. Sauté in oil blend 3 to 4 pieces at a time, cooking (over even heat) just until done. Be careful not to burn caramelized bits that may accumulate on bottom of pan. Place veal on a plate until all is cooked.

Sauce

3 tablespoons olive oil blend   1 cup Marsala wine
½ cup shallot, minced   2 cups browned, veal stock,
2 teaspoons garlic, minced   reduced
½ cup shiitake mushroom caps,   ¼ cup basil, fresh, julienned
  julienned   ⅓ cup dried tomatoes, julienned
½ cup crimini mushrooms, quartered   Salt & black pepper, to taste

Add oil to pan used for cooking veal. Sauté shallots with garlic until translucent; add mushrooms and cook another minute. Deglaze with wine, reducing by two-thirds. Add remaining ingredients. Reduce by one-third over medium high heat. Add cooked veal to sauce, with all juices, until heated through.

Pasta

8 ounces angel hair pasta, fresh   3 tablespoons assorted chopped
3 tablespoons whole butter   herbs (parsley, basil, chives,
1 teaspoon chopped garlic   chervil, oregano)

Toss the just-cooked pasta with remaining ingredients. Place a nest of pasta at top of the plate and shingle 3 pieces of veal in front of it. Coat with sauce.

Yield: 4 servings

Editors' Note: *If shiitake (shee-TAH-kay) or crimini (cri-MEE-nee) mushrooms are unavailable, substitute other varieties. Marsala (mahr-SAH-lah) is an Italian wine. Do not use the cooking variety, sold at supermarkets, at these wines are usually too salty.*

> "For a big night out on the town, pick one of the flowers of Charleston's restaurant garden . . .Blossom Cafe." -- *Southern Living*
>
> "When the revered Magnolias Uptown/Down South opened a spin-off Blossom Cafe, the question isn't whether to try it, but when!"
> --*Town & Country Magazine*

Charleston Chops

Friendly fine dining, a piano bar, and a classy Southern style

Address: 188 East Bay Street
Charleston, SC 29401
(Historic District)
Telephone: (843) 937-9300
Web Site: www.charlestonchops.com

Cuisine: Steak, seafood, and
wild game specialties
Executive Chef: Jeffrey Gibbs
Price Range: Dinner/$18-$26

Bourbon and Ginger Tenderloin Salad

½ cup bourbon
¼ medium red onion
1½ cups soy sauce
1½ tablespoons fresh ginger, peeled and grated

½ tablespoon crushed red pepper
1 cup brown sugar
½ pound beef tenderloin

Combine first 6 ingredients and bring to a boil. Let cool. Add beef and marinate for one hour. Sear over medium-high heat until evenly browned. Let stand for five minutes.

Pear and Ginger Vinaigrette

½ cup fresh pear, peeled and chopped
¾ cup rice vinegar
1 tablespoon Dijon mustard
2 tablespoons fresh, grated ginger
2 tablespoons chopped shallots
1 tablespoon chopped garlic
3 tablespoons soy sauce

Salt and pepper, to taste
1 cup olive oil
4 cups arugula,
washed and sliced
½ medium red onion, sliced
1 pear, cored and sliced

Combine first 8 ingredients in blender. Blend until smooth, slowly adding olive oil. Mix remaining ingredients and let sit for five minutes. Place in center of plates and top with sliced beef.

Yields: 4 servings

Editors' Note: *You may substitute any greens you like for the arugula (ah-ROO-guh-lah), a mustard-flavored green also known as Italian cress, and another meat for the tenderloin.*

Restaurants
Charleston, South Carolina

Smoked Gouda Potato Gratin

½ stick butter
½ small onion, diced
½ tablespoon fresh garlic, minced
3 Yukon gold (boiling) potatoes, thinly sliced

1 cup heavy cream
1 cup Gouda (GOO-dah) cheese, shredded
2 eggs
Salt & pepper, to taste

Melt butter in skillet and caramelize onion with garlic. Mix onion and garlic with potatoes; pour into a shallow 9 x 13-inch pan. Mix remaining ingredients together and pour evenly over potatoes. Cover with topping and bake at 350° for 25 minutes.

Topping

¼ cup ground smoked bacon
1 cup panko (Japanese) bread crumbs
¼ cup shredded gouda

Salt and pepper, to taste
⅛ pound melted butter

Cook bacon until crisp; drain and grind in a food processor. Mix bacon with next 4 ingredients. Slowly mix in melted butter.

Yields: 2-4 servings

Beef Tartare

2 tablespoons garlic
1 tablespoon anchovy paste
2 tablespoons horseradish
2 tablespoons Dijon mustard
2 tablespoons minced capers

1 tablespoon Worcestershire sauce
½ teaspoon Tabasco sauce
Salt and pepper, to taste
1 pound filet mignon
Brioche, crackers, or toast points

Combine first 8 ingredients. Cut filet into fine diced pieces and mix 30 minutes before serving. Tightly wrap and refrigerate. Serve with brioche (BREE-ohsh), crackers, or toast points.

Yields: 4 servings

Editors' Notes: *Use only top-quality beef for this dish. Beef/Steak Tartare (tar-TAR) is served, uncooked, in the tradition of the Tartars who inhabited the Baltic provinces of medieval Russia. This dish is often offered, as an appetizer, at fine dining steak houses. For an impressive presentation, prepare tartare in a ring mold and garnish with capers, chopped parsley, sliced red onions, and Asiago cheese.*

"Chops is tops."--*City Paper* (July 2000)

"A first-class steakhouse."--*Post & Courier* (12-24-98)

"A jazzy interior with Southern style."--*Post & Courier* (April 2003)

Cypress Cowcountry Grille

Charleston's hottest new place to dine

Address: 167 East Bay Street
Charleston, SC 29401
(Historic District)
Telephone: (843) 727-0111 x 1
E-mail: reservations@magnolias-blossom-cypress.com
Web Site: www.magnolias-blossom-cypress.com

Cuisine: Classic American
cuisine with an Asian flair
Executive Chef: Craig Deihl
Price Range: Dinner/$17–$36

Tuna & Oysters on Half Shell with Cilantro

2 tablespoons chopped cilantro
¼ cup freshly-squeezed lime juice
3 tablespoons rice wine vinegar
3 tablespoons honey
1 teaspoon salt

10 fresh oysters in shell
(scrubbed free of dirt and debris)
½ pound sashimi-grade tuna
1 cup rock salt
Cilantro leaves

Combine the first five ingredients in a small mixing bowl and incorporate evenly. Place in the refrigerator to chill. Using an oyster knife, shuck oysters and remove top shell. Leaving the oyster in the half shell, rinse with water to remove any remaining grit. Using a sharp knife, cut tuna into 10 thin strips (approximately ⅛–inch thick) and place on top of the oysters. Place 1 teaspoon of refrigerated glaze on top of each oyster. On a plate, place 1 cup of rock salt and top with cilantro leaves (the rock salt keeps the oysters from sliding around). Place oysters on top of cilantro and rock salt; serve immediately.

Yield: 2 servings

Editors' Notes: *Sometimes placing meat (such as tuna in this recipe) in a freezer for up to 20 minutes makes it easier to slice thin. Sashimi (sah-SHEE-mee) is a fish served raw with condiments.. Since it is served raw, it must be fresh and top-quality. Cilantro, also known as coriander and Chinese parsley, can usually be found year-round in most supermarkets. Rice wine vinegar can be found with other vinegars in supermarket or at an Asian market.*

❧❧❧❧❧❧❧❧❧❧❧❧❧❧❧❧❧❧❧❧❧❧❧❧❧❧❧❧

Seared Wahoo Over Truffle Grits
Wahoo

10 ounces fresh wahoo
   (can substitute grouper, snapper or halibut)
Salt and pepper to taste
2 ounces olive oil
2 ounces butter
6 large local white shrimp (peeled and deveined)
2 tablespoons thinly sliced garlic cloves
3 tablespoons thinly sliced shallots

1 cup asparagus tips
3 ounces white wine
3 ounces butter (cold)
½ cup grape tomatoes, sliced in half
3 tablespoons fresh basil, chopped
1 teaspoon salt
Pinch of white pepper

Cut fish into 2 equal-size pieces; season with salt and pepper. Sear wahoo (in hot olive oil in a sauté pan) over medium-high heat 2 to 3 minutes. Flip fish and add next 4 ingredients. Continue to cook 2 to 3 minutes, then remove fish from pan. Add asparagus to pan and cook 1 to 2 minutes. Remove shrimp from pan and deglaze pan with white wine; reduce liquid by half (takes approximately 2 minutes). Over low heat, stir in butter until melted and creamy. Add remaining ingredients. To assemble, place wahoo on top of a serving of Truffle Grits and surround with three shrimp. Next, place equal amounts of asparagus and tomato mixture on top of fish. Spoon sauce around the fish.

Yield: 2 servings

Editors' Note: *Grape tomatoes are baby Roma tomatoes.*

Truffle Grits

3 cups of water
1 cup white grits, preferably stone ground
3 tablespoons butter
¼ cup heavy cream

1-2 teaspoons truffle oil
1½ tablespoons salt
½ teaspoon ground white pepper
1½ tablespoons honey

Bring water to boil. Stir in grits and cook 25 to 30 minutes over medium-low heat until water is absorbed; grits should be slightly creamy. Add remaining ingredients and cook another 5 to 10 minutes.

Yield: 2-4 servings

Editors' Notes: *Truffles, an edible fungi considered a delicacy, have been proclaimed (since ancient times) to have therapeutic and aphrodisiac powers. Truffle oil is available in gourmet or specialty shops. The flavor is strong, so you may want to consider adding a little at a time.*

"In opening Cypress, they have raised the bar for Charleston restaurants. This is a special place." --Charleston's *Post & Courier* (2002)

"Best New Restaurants-2001," *Esquire Magazine*
Wine Spectator "Award of Excellence" winner since 2001

Hominy Grill

Charleston's favorite neighborhood restaurant

Address: 207 Rutledge Avenue
Charleston, SC 29403
(Historic District)
Telephone: (843) 937-0930
Web Site: www.hominygrill.com

Cuisine: Southern cooking
Executive Chef: Robert Stehling
Price Range: Breakfast/$2.75~$5.75
Lunch/$3.25~$6.75
Dinner/$8.50~$17.25

Southern Fried Chicken

1 (3-pound) chicken, cut up
1 cup buttermilk
2 cups peanut oil

1 cup all-purpose flour
2 teaspoons salt
Freshly ground black pepper

Marinate chicken in buttermilk 2 to 24 hours. Preheat peanut oil in cast-iron skillet. While oil is preheating, combine dry ingredients in a paper bag; drop chicken pieces into the bag, tossing to coat evenly (be careful not to over-flour). Hold each piece up and shake off excess flour. Place chicken in hot skillet, skin side down, with about one-half inch of oil. Add dark pieces to skillet first, followed by white pieces. Chicken should start frying immediately. After a minute or so, turn heat down to medium low. Leave chicken alone, agitating it only enough to make sure it is not sticking to the pan. When chicken starts turning white and juices are oozing out, flip to cook other side. It should be about two-thirds cooked at this time. If the heat is too high and the chicken is flipped too soon, the crust will fall off. Finish frying and set chicken pieces on a platter to rest for 5 minutes. After checking doneness, by making a small cut in bottom of chicken, remove chicken to paper towels to drain.

Yield: 5-6 servings

Editors' Notes: *We used skinless, boneless chicken breasts, and they were excellent!*

Restaurants
Charleston, South Carolina

Okra Beignets

½ cup jasmine rice, cooked
2 cups fresh okra, sliced
½ green pepper, diced
1 onion, diced

1 egg
¼ cup heavy cream
½ cup all-purpose flour
Canola oil, enough for deep frying

Cook rice, according to directions. Let cool. Combine next 6 ingredients and let set for at least 20 minutes. Mixture will become slimy from okra. Add drained rice to ingredients. Spoon mixture into frying pan, with hot canola, and deep fry until brown on each side. Drain well and serve.

Yield: 12-15 beignets

Editors' Notes: *Jasmine rice can be found at most supermarkets or at an Asian food market. Beignets (ben-YAYS) is a derivative of the French word meaning "fritter" and are especially popular in New Orleans in other variations. Cooked, chopped shrimp is also excellent added to the beignets. If shrimp is desired, stir in after adding the rice.*

Saffron Rice Croquettes

White Sauce
Use your favorite white sauce recipe and season (to taste) with 1 bay leaf, red pepper flakes, nutmeg, butter, salt and white pepper. Stir in ½ cup onion, julienned.

Croquettes

1½ cups jasmine rice
Pinch of saffron
½ cup white sauce, chilled
2½ tablespoons fresh parsley, chives,and/or basil (finely chopped)
¼ cup Parmesan cheese, grated

⅛ cup sweet red pepper, sautéed till tender
Salt, white pepper, & Tabasco sauce, to taste
½ cup plain bread crumbs
Peanut oil for frying

Cook rice, according to directions, with saffron. Drain rice and stir in white sauce, fresh herbs, Parmesan cheese, and red pepper. Season with salt, pepper, and Tabasco. Roll mixture into walnut-sized nuggets, dredge in bread crumbs, and deep fry until brown and crispy. Drain and serve hot.

Yield: 8-10 croquettes

"Where the Biscuits Meet the Gravy."
--*New York Times*, April 26, 2000

"If you want to have an excellent meal in a cozy inviting Charleston single house where you can hold a conversation, Hominy Grill is the place."

Joseph's

Family-operated and a favorite with the locals

Address: 129 Meeting Street
Charleston, SC 29401
(Historic District)
Telephone: (843) 958-8500
Web Site: www.josephsofcharleston.com

Cuisine: American eclectic
Executive Chef: Joseph Passarini
Price Range: Breakfast/$5.50-$8.95
Lunch/$5-$12
(Only breakfast served on Sundays)

Joseph's Spinach and Artichoke Soup

Roux

¼ cup butter   ¼ cup all-purpose flour

Cook butter and flour together in a small saucepan, over medium heat, for 5 to 10 minutes until there is a nutty smell. Set roux (ROO) aside.

Soup

1 teaspoon garlic, chopped
½ medium yellow onion, diced
Olive oil, as needed
1 (8-ounce) packages frozen chopped
   spinach, defrosted and drained
1½ cups artichoke hearts, save liquid
1 bay leaf
½ teaspoon fresh thyme, chopped

½ teaspoon fresh basil, chopped
½ teaspoon fresh rosemary, chopped
½ cup water
1(16-ounce) can chicken broth
½ cup heavy cream
1 tablespoon grated Romano cheese
Salt and pepper, to taste

In a saucepan, sauté garlic and onion in olive oil until onion is tender. Add next 2 ingredients, saving liquid from artichokes. Cook for 5 minutes. Add herbs, artichoke juice, water, and chicken broth. Bring to a boil, then lower to a simmer. Add roux, stirring with a whisk. Once roux is blended into mixture, add remaining ingredients.

Yield: 4-6 servings

Fried Green Tomatoes with Sweet Citrus Rémoulade

Dust

2 cups all-purpose flour
1 teaspoon salt
1 teaspoon black pepper

½ teaspoon cayenne pepper
1 teaspoon garlic powder
1 teaspoon onion powder

Blend together and set aside.

Tomatoes

4 large green tomatoes,
    cut into thick slices
1 cup flour

3 whole eggs, beaten
4 cups dust
Vegetable oil, for frying

Dust tomatoes in plain flour, in eggs, then into dust. Fry at 350° until golden brown. Drain on paper and serve hot with rémoulade.

Editors' Note: *Green tomatoes are seasonal and available during the spring and summer months.*

Sweet Citrus Rémoulade

2 cups mayonnaise
1 teaspoon Worcestershire sauce
Pinch of salt and pepper
2 tablespoons lemon juice
1 teaspoon paprika

1 tablespoon green sweet relish
Handful of fresh parsley
1 tablespoon grained mustard
1 tablespoon capers

Put all ingredients into food processor and blend for about 30 seconds. Chill.

Yield: 4 servings

"Unpretentious...superb."
— *The New York Times*

"Breakfast and lunch never tasted so good."
— *The Post and Courier*

Featured on the *Food Network*, October 2002

———————————

The Passarini family takes great pride in the quality, consistency, and honesty of their food and service.

Magnolia's

A unique blend of historic charm and contemporary excitement

Address: 185 E. Bay Street
Charleston, SC 29402
(Historic District)
Telephone: (843) 577-7771
Web Site: www.magnolias-blossom-cypress.com

Cuisine: New Southern cuisine
Executive Chef: Donald Drake
Price Range: Lunch/$7-$16
Dinner/$18-$28
Cookbook: *Magnolias Uptown/
Down South Southern Cuisine*

Creamy Tomato Bisque with Lump Crabmeat

2 tablespoons extra virgin olive oil
¼ cup yellow onion, chopped
½ teaspoon garlic, minced
¼ cup flour
1½ cups chicken broth, divided
½ chicken bouillon cube
2 cups homemade tomato sauce
  or 1 (4½-ounce) can of tomato sauce
1 cup tomato juice

1½ large peeled fresh vine ripened
  tomatoes or 1 (8-ounce) can whole
  peeled tomatoes, crushed with juice
½ cup thinly sliced fresh basil,
  loosely packed (save ⅛ cup for garnish)
½ cup heavy cream
¼ teaspoon salt
Dash of white pepper
4 ounces fresh lump crabmeat, picked clean

Heat olive oil over medium heat in a heavy-bottomed stockpot. Add next 2 ingredients and sauté for 2 to 3 minutes, stirring until onions are translucent. Reduce heat and make a roux by adding flour and stirring until well-blended. Continue cooking over low heat for 5 minutes, stirring constantly. Turn heat up to medium and add ¾ cups of broth, stirring vigorously. Stir constantly until broth begins thickening and is smooth. Gradually add remaining broth and bouillon cube, stirring constantly until broth re-thickens. Reduce heat to low and simmer 5 minutes to cook out starchy flavor. Add next 4 ingredients and simmer 10 minutes. Skim off any foam collected on the top; add cream. Bring to a simmer and skim again, if necessary. Taste and add salt and pepper, if needed. When ready to serve, warm soup bowls. Garnish by sprinkling crabmeat and remaining basil over soup. Serve immediately.

Yield: 4 (10-ounce) servings

Editors' Note: *This bisque (bihsk) is also good without the crabmeat and flavored with gin.*

ᘒᘒᘒᘒᘒᘒᘒᘒᘒᘒᘒᘒᘒᘒᘒᘒᘒᘒᘒᘒᘒᘒᘒᘒᘒᘒ

Carpaccio of Fried Green Tomatoes

Tomato Chutney

1 cup onions, julienned	3 cups Roma tomatoes,
2 cups cider vinegar	julienned with seeds removed
2 cups sugar	1 tablespoons red pepper flakes

Combine all ingredients. Set aside.

Tomatoes

1 egg, beaten	1 cup seasoned flour
1 cup buttermilk	2 cups panko bread crumbs
Tabasco sauce, to taste	3 cups fry oil
12 green tomatoes, thinly sliced	

Beat first 3 ingredients in a bowl. Dip tomato slices in flour; shake off. Place tomato slices in buttermilk mixture and coat with bread crumbs. Fry in hot oil until brown.

Tomato Salad

1 cup cherry tomatoes	½ cup yellow pepper,	½ cup red wine vinegar
1 cup yellow tear drops	julienned	Salt and pepper to taste
1 cup Dixie Dew drops	1 tablespoon garlic	Goat cheese, crumbled
½ cup red onion, julienned	½ cup olive oil	½ cup fresh basil, chopped

Combine all ingredients, saving some cheese and basil for garnish.

Assembly

Place tomato chutney in center of plate. Top with 3 fried tomato slices and a generous serving of tomato salad. Garnish with cheese and basil.

Yield: 4 servings

Editors' Notes: *This carpaccio (kahr-PAH-chee-oh) is a medley of delicious tomatoes. Yellow tear drops and Dixie Dew drops are regional variations of the cherry tomato (which may be used alone, in the salad, if the other ones are unavailable). For a "peppier" flavor, add extra Tabasco sauce; add extra red pepper flakes (in chutney) if you like a hot and spicey taste. Do not use a substitute for panko bread crumbs (available in Asian markets and some supermarkets) as they make all the difference in the breading.*

"Magnolia's--perhaps the city's most celebrated restaurant."
--- *Southern Living*

"Magnolia's a smart uptown space, specializes in updated Southern Food."
---*The New York Times*

"The hot spot in town . . .the restaurant is contemporary and upbeat."
-- *Detroit Free Press*

McCrady's

*McCrady's perfectly combines Charleston's love of history
with its hunger for new ideas*

Address: 2 Unity Alley
Charleston, SC 29401
(Historic District)
Telephone: (843) 577-0025

Web Site: www.mccradysrestaurant.com
Cuisine: Contemporary American
Executive Chef: Michael Kramer
Price Range: Dinner/$18-$29

Hearts of Palm Salad

Walnut Vinaigrette

¼ cup Dijon mustard
⅛ cup honey
¾ cup red wine vinegar
¼ cup lemon juice

½ cup walnut oil
1 cup canola oil
1 teaspoon finely chopped rosemary
Salt and pepper, to taste

In medium-sized mixing bowl, briskly whisk together first 4 ingredients. Cntinue whisking and slowly drizzle in oils until emulsified. Add remaining ingredients. Set aside.

Salad

½ pound mixed baby lettuces
Salt and pepper, to taste
¼ pound fresh hearts of palm, blanched
½ cup chèvre (goat cheese), crumbled

½ cup candied walnuts
¼ cup cucumber (seeded and sliced
into ¼-inch pieces), optional

Dress greens well; season with salt and pepper. Place greens on plate, top with hearts of palm, sprinkle with chèvre, candied walnuts, and cucumber.

Yield: 4 servings

Editors' Notes: *Walnut oil can usually be found in gourmet shops. It is expensive, but it is an integral part of this recipe and can be kept in the refrigerator indefinitely. Candied walnuts are sometimes available in food specialty shops. However, you may make your own by using the "Candied Pecans" recipe on page 94 and substituting walnuts for the pecans.*

❧❧❧❧❧❧❧❧❧❧❧❧❧❧❧❧❧❧❧❧❧❧❧❧❧❧

Grilled Veal Tenderloin

Sauce

4 cups red wine	Salt and pepper, to taste
4 tablespoons sugar	2 tablespoons butter, softened
2 tablespoons Madeira	

Place first 2 ingredients in a small saucepan over medium heat. Reduce to approximately 1 cup, or until mixture coats back of spoon. Stir in Madeira, over heat, for another minute. Then add remaining ingredients. Set aside and keep warm.

Vegetables

2 tablespoons butter	8 red potatoes, roasted
2 large portabello mushrooms, cut into 1-inch pieces	2 sweet potatoes, peeled, cut into 1-inch cubes and roasted
1 bunch asparagus tips, blanched	Salt and pepper, to taste

Melt butter in a large saucepan. Add mushrooms and cook until soft, about 3 minutes. Add remaining vegetables; season with salt and pepper. Set aside and keep warm.

Veal

4 (6-ounce) veal steaks	Salt and pepper, to taste

Heat grill to medium-high heat. Season all sides of veal well with salt and pepper. Place on grill at "10 o'clock" position; after 3 minutes, turn to "2 o'clock" position to achieve a criss-cross pattern. Turn veal over and repeat. Set aside and keep warm. To serve, place vegetables on center of the plate with sauce around the vegetables. Center veal on top.

Yield: 4 servings

Editors' note: *The "10 o'clock" and "2 o'clock" positions refer to the arrangement of veal on grill for marking purposes (i.e., to develop criss-cross grill marks on the steaks). This wine sauce is also good served over veal medallions or scaloppine.*

Recipient of the prestigious Dirona Award (2004)

Named by Charleston's *Post and Courier* as "Restaurant of the Year" (2002)

Featured as one of *Esquire Magazine's* "Best New Restaurants of 1999."

Built in 1778, McCrady's is housed within one of the oldest existing taverns in the United States. During George Washington's southern tour in 1791, a party was held for him in The Longroom.

Middleton Place

Dining with spectacular views of the gardens at world-famous Middleton Place

Address: 4300 Ashley River Road
Charleston, SC 29414
Telephone: (843) 556-6020
E-mail: restaurant@middletonplace.org
Web Site: www.middletonplace.org/restaurant.htm

Cuisine: Lowcountry plantation fare
Executive Chef: Tim Bedwell
Price Range: Lunch/$5.95-$12.95
Dinner/$15.95-$21.95
(Reservations required)

Warm Turkey Salad

Vinaigrette Dressing

⅔ cup olive oil
⅓ cup apple cider vinegar
1 teaspoon salt
1 teaspoon sugar
½ teaspoon ground black pepper
½ teaspoon dry mustard
1 garlic clove, minced

1 teaspoon onion, minced
⅓ cup celery stalk, minced
½ green bell pepper, minced
½ red bell pepper minced
2 teaspoons parsley flakes
½ teaspoon thyme

Mix all ingredients together.

Salad

1 turkey breast
Vinaigrette dressing
Mixed greens

Small bunch of grapes, red or green
½ cup pecans, chopped

Roast turkey breast and cool. Pull turkey apart. Marinate turkey in vinaigrette dressing and heat slowly. Serve over mixed greens topped with grapes and chopped pecans.

Yield: 6-8 servings

Restaurants
Charleston, South Carolina

❦❦❦❦❦❦❦❦❦❦❦❦❦❦❦❦❦❦❦❦

Corn Pudding

2 cups fresh yellow corn

2 whole eggs

3 cups heavy cream

¼ teaspoon nutmeg

Pinch of salt and white pepper

Place yellow corn in a greased casserole pan. Mix all other ingredients together. Pour mixture over corn and bake for 45 minutes at 350° or until golden brown.

Yield: 6-8 servings

Editors' Note: *Goes well with turkey and ham at Thanksgiving.*

Huguenot Torte

3 whole eggs

2 cups sugar

1 cup flour

½ teaspoon baking powder

½ teaspoon salt

4 Granny Smith apples, chopped

4 cups pecans chopped

½ teaspoon vanilla extract

Whipped cream, optional

Beat eggs until frothy and lemon colored. Add remaining ingredients and mix well. Pour into a greased sheet pan and bake at 325° for 15 to 20 minutes.

Yield: 8-10 servings

Editors' Notes: *Granny Smith apples are characterized by a freckled green skin. It is sweetly tart with a moderately juicy flesh. Huguenot Torte (TOHRT) is yummy served with whipped cream and festive garnished with a sprig of mint.*

Middleton Place, a National Historic Landmark and carefully preserved 18th-century plantation, has survived the American Revolution, the Civil War, earthquakes, and hurricanes. It has been home to many generations of the Middleton family beginning with Henry Middleton, President of the First Continental Congress; his son Arthur, a signer of the Declaration of Independence; his grandson Henry, Governor of South Carolina and an American Minister to Russia; and his great-grandson William, a signer of the Ordinance of Secession. Today the plantation (including extensive gardens, the plantation stables, and the house museum) is owned and operated by Middleton Place Foundation.

Poogan's Porch

Charleston's oldest award-winning restaurant

Address: 72 Queen Street
Charleston, SC 29402
(Historic District)
Telephone: (843) 577-2337
Web Site: www.poogansporch.com

Cuisine: Lowcountry cuisine
Executive Chef: Nick Spondike
Price Range: Brunch/$4.25-$8.95
Lunch/$5.95-$9.95
Dinner/$13.95-$23.95

Stuffed Carolina Quail

1 cup spinach, wilted in butter
4 ounces smoked Gouda cheese
6 oven-roasted shallots

4 semi-boneless quail
2 tablespoons extra virgin olive oil
½ cup seasoned flour

Combine first 3 ingredients. Divide mixture into four portions and stuff into body cavity of quail. Brush each bird, liberally, with extra virgin olive oil and lightly dredge in flour. In a hot pan, sear quail on both sides to achieve a golden crust. Transfer to a 425° oven and roast approximately 8 to 10 minutes or until firm to touch.

Yield: 2 servings

Editors' Notes: *Superb served upon a bed of garlic whipped potatoes, accompanied by your favorite sautéed vegetable. A rich sauce, incorporating red wine and reduced brown stock, provides the crowning touch for this dish.*

Restaurants
Charleston, South Carolina

❦❦❦❦❦❦❦❦❦❦❦❦❦❦❦❦❦❦❦❦❦❦❦❦

Walnut Encrusted Stuffed Chicken

4 boneless, skinless chicken breasts
2 cloves fresh garlic, minced
1 cup yellow onion, diced
4 ounces smoked ham, diced
1 cup mushrooms, diced
1 stick unsalted butter
1 bunch fresh chives, chopped

2 tablespoons fresh parsley, chopped
1 cup dry white wine
1 cup heavy cream
1 cup flour
2 eggs, well beaten
2 cups walnuts, crushed
2 cups canola oil

Using a meat mallet, pound chicken breasts to achieve uniform thickness; set aside. In a medium pan, sauté next 4 ingredients in butter. When onions become translucent, add next 4 ingredients and simmer, briefly, to reduce wine and further intensify flavors. Slowly incorporate flour and continue stirring until mixture thickens. Remove stuffing mixture from heat and set aside to cool. Place a heaping tablespoon of stuffing on each chicken breast; roll breast, while tucking in the ends, to form a pocket. Using a standard breading technique, dredge breasts into flour, egg wash (beaten eggs plus 1 tablespoon water), and the crushed walnuts. Heat oil in a cast iron pan to approximately 350°. Pan fry breasts on all sides to achieve a crisp, golden texture. Place in a 400° oven and continue cooking until done.

Yield: 4 servings

Editors' Notes: *The chicken breasts may be prepared, in advance, and refrigerated until time to cook them. Try serving this dish with rice or polenta. A simple cream sauce, flavored with chicken broth and a few mushrooms, makes a great addition.*

"Poogan's Porch is about Southern favorites,
big portions, reasonable prices, and authentic charm.
--The Post and Courier

"Once you've tasted the food at Poogan's Porch,
you'll understand why magazines like
Bon Appetit, Gourmet, and *Cuisine*
have requested their recipes."
--TravelHost Magazine

Slightly North of Broad

Distinguished from the crowd by its decor and approach to food

Address: 192 East Bay Street
Charleston, SC 29401
(Historic District)
Telephone: (843) 723-3424
Web Site: www.slightlynorthofbroad.net

Cuisine: Maverick Lowcountry
Executive Chef: Frank Lee
Price Range: Lunch/$7-$12
Dinner/$10-$22

S.N.O.B.'s Award-Winning Maverick Grits
Grits

4 cups water
1 tablespoon butter
½ teaspoon salt

1-1½ cups stone ground grits
¼ cup cream

Bring first 3 ingredients to a boil. Stir in grits. Reduce heat to low and cook, stirring occasionally, until grits are thick and creamy (approximately 40 minutes). Remove from heat. Stir in cream and additional butter, if desired. Keep warm.

Topping

1 tablespoon butter
4 ounces country ham, julienned
4 ounces smoked pork sausage, cut in circles
(may substitute andouille or other spicy sausage)
12 shrimp, peeled and deveined
8 sea scallops, fresh or "dry pack"

2 cloves fresh garlic, minced
Pinch of Cajun spice
¼ cup tablespoons green onion, diced
¼ cup fresh tomato, seeded and diced
1 tablespoon water
1 additional tablespoon butter

Sauté ham and sausage in 1 tablespoon butter. Add shrimp and scallops and sauté for 1 to 2 minutes. Add next 2 ingredients and sauté 30 seconds; stir in next 2 ingredients. Add remaining ingredients, scraping browned bits on bottom of pan (makes a delicious sauce for coating the shrimp, scallops, ham, and sausage). Spoon grits onto plates in equal portions. Place 2 scallops and 3 shrimp, per person, on grits and spoon equal parts of topping per plate.

Yield: 4 servings

Editors' Note: *We recomment using "dry pack" scallops, though harder to find, as they acatually brown when sautéed. This recipe is a melding of two favorite Lowcountry dishes-- Lowcountry Boil and Shrimp & Grits—this recipe was selected by GQ Magazine for a "Golden Dish" award in 1994.*

ক্ষ-ক্ষ-ক্ষ-ক্ষ-ক্ষ-ক্ষ-ক্ষ-ক্ষ-ক্ষ-ক্ষ-ক্ষ-ক্ষ-ক্ষ-ক্ষ-ক্ষ-ক্ষ-ক্ষ-ক্ষ-ক্ষ-ক্ষ

Deviled Crab Cakes

1¾ pounds crab claw meat	2 whole eggs	¼ tablespoon pepper
½ medium green bell pepper	½ cup half-and-half	2 tablespoons yellow mustard
½ medium red bell pepper	½ cup cracker meal	¾ teaspoon Tabasco
½ medium red onion	¼ tablespoon salt	2 tablespoons lemon juice

Pick claw meat clean, and mix together all ingredients. Let sit refrigerated for 20 minutes, allowing time for cracker meal to absorb moisture. Form cakes and roll in cracker meal; deep fry or sauté in canola oil.

Yields: 14-16 medium crab cakes

Key Lime Tart with Passion Fruit Sauce
Crust

1½ sticks softened margarine	Pinch of salt	1 cup of chopped pecans
5 tablespoons 10-X sugar	2 teaspoons ice water	1 10-inch springform pan
2 cups all purpose flour	2 teaspoons vanilla	

Combine first 2 ingredients and blend well. Sift together flour and salt. Combine ice water with vanilla. Alternating, add first one-third of flour to sugar mixture. Then add one-third of water mixture. Continue adding, alternately, until all flour and water mixture are used. Stir in chopped pecans; dough will be crumbly. Chill for 15 minutes. Remove dough from and roll between two sheets of wax paper to a thickness of ¼-inch. Lay crust into the pan and bake at 350 degrees until light brown, approximately 20 minutes. When crust is light brown, remove from oven and pour filling into crust. Continue baking at 350° for 10 more minutes. Remove from oven to wire rack to cool. Chill before serving.

Filling

24 ounces Eagle Brand Condensed milk	Zest (grated peel) of 2 limes
⅔ cup Nellie & Joe's Key lime juice	5 egg yolks, beaten together

Mix milk with juice and zest. Stir in egg yolks. Set aside until crust is ready

Passion Fruit Sauce

½ cup water	½ cup passion fruit purée	⅛ teaspoon ground ginger
⅛ cup pineapple juice	(about 1 passion fruit)	1 tablespoons cornstarch
1 cups sugar	Pinch of salt	

Combine ¼ cup water with next 3 ingredients; bring to a rolling boil. Add last 3 ingredients and return to a boil. Dissolve cornstarch in remaining ⅛ cup water and add to boiling mixture. Cook and stir until thickened; strain and chill. Drizzle over tart.

Editors' Note: *Passion fruit, also known as granadilla or star fruit, is available in supermarkets on a seasonal basis. It is irreplaceable in this scrumptious fruit sauce!*

"Contemporary Southern cooking is the buzz phrase at a number of restaurants contributing to Charleston's increasingly sophisticated dining scene... standouts include Slightly North of Broad." *--USA Today* (5/14/1999)

Long Point Inn

*Overlooking a scenic marsh and next door to Boone Hall Plantation,
Long Point Inn offers a refreshing Lowcountry B&B experience.*

Address: 1199 Long Point Road
Mount Pleasant, SC 29464
Telephone: (843) 849-1884
E-mail: info@Charleston–
LongPtInn.com

Web Site: www.charleston–
longptinn.com
Category: B&B
Proprietress: Catharine Jennings
Rates: $89-$179 (seasonal)

Cheese-Laced Hash Browns

1 package of shredded hash browns
1 can cream of celery soup
8 ounces shredded Cheddar cheese

¾ cup sour cream
½ stick butter, melted
¾ cup onion

Spray (or grease with butter) a 2-quart glass baking dish. Combine all ingredients and spread in baking dish. Bake in a 350 ° oven for 45 minutes to 1 hour.

Yield: 8-10 servings

Editors' Note: *Add 1 pound of browned ground beef and top with additional cheese to create a main dish meal.*

Bed & Breakfasts and Historic Inns
Mt. Pleasant, South Carolina
୬୬୬୬୬୬୬୬୬୬୬୬୬୬୬୬୬୬୬୬୬୬୬

Charleston Cheese Soufflé

3 cups fresh, untoasted white bread cubes
1 cup fresh or frozen chopped onion
Salt and pepper
1½ Cheddar cheese, grated
1½ cups milk

4 eggs, beaten
1 tablespoon Worcestershire sauce
2 tablespoons yellow mustard
3 tomatoes, thinly sliced
3 tablespoons butter, sliced

Spray an 8½ x 11-inch glass baking dish with baking spray or grease with butter. Combine bread cubes, onion, salt and pepper with 1 cup of cheese. Spread into baking dish. Combine milk with next 3 ingredients; mix well. Pour egg mixture over ingredients in baking dish and sprinkle with remaining cheese. Arrange tomato slices on top of soufflé (soo-FLAY) and dot with sliced butter. Bake in a 325° oven for 1 hour.

Yield: 6 servings

Editors' Note: *An egg substitute may be used instead of eggs, and the soufflé may be prepared in advance and refrigerated overnight. Delicious served with cured ham!*

"This Charleston inn is new among the old--nestled amongst a stand of 300 year old live oak trees, it is the perfect setting for a quality Bed and Breakfast right in the middle of one of the most historical sections in America." --*Gwinette Daily Post*

Long Point Inn, built upon historic property once part of Snee Farm Plantation and owned by Charles Pinckney (a signer of The Constitution), became part of Boone Hall Plantation after being sold to Governor Alexander Stone. The marsh front served as prosperous rice fields.

Price House Cottage

This National Register property lies in the heart of Summerville's Historic District

Address: 224 Sumter Avenue
Summerville, SC 29483
Telephone: (843) 871-1877
E–mail: phcbb@aol.com

Web Site: www.pricehousecottage.com
Category: B&B
Owners/Innkeepers: Jennifer & David Price
Rate: $145 (year-round)

Pumpkin Belgian Waffles with Vermont Maple Syrup Whipped Cream

(Adapted from *Morning Glories*, by Donna Leahy)

2 cups all-purpose flour
¼ cup sugar
4 teaspoons baking powder
1 teaspoon salt
1 teaspoon cinnamon
1 teaspoon ginger

¼ teaspoon cloves
1½ cups milk
1 cup pumpkin purée, canned
4 eggs, separated
1 cup butter, melted

Preheat waffle iron (Belgian or regular). In a large bowl, combine first 7 ingredients. Whisk together the next 2 ingredients plus egg yolks. Stir pumpkin mixture into the dry ingredients and add melted butter. Beat egg whites until stiff and fold into pumpkin mixture. Ladle batter onto waffle iron and cook until steam ceases to escape from the iron, producing a lightly browned waffle.

Flavored Whipping Cream

1 cup whipping cream   2 tablespoons pure maple syrup

Whip cream until peaks begin to appear. Add syrup. Continue whipping the cream until stiff peaks form. Serve waffles with pure maple syrup and a generous scoop of the flavored whipped cream.

Yield: 6

Editors' Notes: *Add chopped pecans to this batter and cook as pancakes--ideal during the Thanksgiving season!*

Bed & Breakfasts and Historic Inns
Summerville, South Carolina

๑๑๑๑๑๑๑๑๑๑๑๑๑๑๑๑๑๑๑๑๑๑๑๑๑๑๑๑๑๑๑๑

Artichoke Baked Eggs

(Adapted from *The New Basics Cookbook* by Rosso and Lukins)

1 medium tomato,
   sliced ¼ inch thick, peeled and seeded
¼ teaspoon salt
2 tablespoons unsalted butter
8 ounces lean ham, cubed
2 tablespoons freshly grated
   Parmesan cheese

4 artichoke hearts, thinly
   sliced lengthwise. Use canned,
   but not marinated, artichoke hearts.
3 tablespoons sour cream
4 eggs, separated
Freshly ground pepper to taste
Chopped fresh parsley to garnish

Preheat oven to 450° and place pot of water on stove to boil. Slice, peel, and seed tomato; place between paper towels to absorb moisture. Sauté ham in 1 tablespoon unsalted butter until slightly browned. Remove to paper towel to absorb any liquid. Place half the ham in each of the bottoms of two oval 9 x 5 x 2-inch ramekins. Place tomato slices over ham to cover in single thickness. Sprinkle with Parmesan cheese and salt. Place the artichoke slices evenly over cheese and cover with sour cream. Spread sour cream evenly and place two indentations on each preparation with back of a spoon that has been run under hot water. Place the egg yolks in the indentations. In a small bowl break up the egg whites with a fork so that they will flow as a liquid; do not beat the whites. Pour this mixture into the ramekins, being careful to keep the egg whites from running over the edge of the ramekins. Place ½ tablespoon of unsalted butter on top of each ramekin. Place the ramekins in a shallow roasting pan (or Pyrex baking dish) for a water bath. Fill with boiling water to reach approximately ⅖ the way up the ramekins. Bake for 11 minutes. Remove from the water bath and place ramekins on individual plates. Sprinkle with freshly ground pepper and garnish with freshly chopped parsley. There will be a small amount of liquid on top of the ramekin at the end of cooking. This is melted butter and not uncooked egg.

Yield: 2 servings

Editors' Notes: *One of our recipe testers suggests chopping the tomato into ½–inch cubes, using a 5" x 3" x 2" ramekin, and baking for 16 minutes. or until egg whites are opaque. For individuals who do not care for "runny" eggs, scrambling the eggs (and pouring over layers of ham, cheese, tomatoes, and artichokes) is recommended. This variation would need to be cooked for 30 to 40 minutes in a 325 degree oven.*

Featured on cover of *The INNside Scoop's* Winter 1999-2000 edition.

━━━━━━━━━━━━━━

One of the earliest houses in Summerville, the main house was built as a summer retreat from Charleston's heat and humidity. The cottage, a former servant's quarters at the rear of the property, is a past recipient of the Summerville Preservation Society Restoration Award.

Rice Hope Plantation

A 17th century rice plantation where time is still marked by the tides in the river.

Address: 206 Rice Hope Drive
Moncks Corner, SC 29461
Reservations: 1-800-569-4038
Telephone: (843) 761-4832
E–mail: lou@ricehope.com

Web Site: www.ricehope.com
Category: B&B
Proprietor: Lou Edens
Innkeepers: Jamie & Katie Edens
Rates: $85-$165 (year-round)

Rosebud Farms Fruit Dish

5-6 Golden Delicious apples
1 (16-ounce) can cranberry sauce

1 (8-ounce) can crushed pineapple,
    drained

Peel, core, and dice apples. Add cranberry sauce and pineapple. Pour into a 9 x 13-inch baking dish; cover and refrigerate overnight. Bring to room temperature. Add topping.

Topping

¼ cup flour
⅓ cup brown sugar
½ cup raw oatmeal

½ teaspoon cinnamon
¼ cup butter

Mix all topping ingredients and sprinkle on top of fruit. Bake at 350° for 45 minutes. Serve hot or cold.

Yield: 8 servings

Editors' Notes: *Use cranberry sauce with whole berries. This is a good fruit choice to serve during the fall and winter months.*

ఆఆఆఆఆఆఆఆఆఆఆఆఆఆఆఆఆఆఆఆ

Cheesy Grits & Sausage Casserole

2 pounds sausage, cooked & drained	1 (6-ounce) package cornbread mix
½ pound grated cheese	1½ cups milk, heated
4 eggs, beaten	½ cup butter, melted
1 cup cooked grits	¾ teaspoon salt

Grease 9 x 13-inch baking dish. Layer sausage and half of the cheese on bottom of dish. Mix eggs and next 5 ingredients. Pour over sausage mixture and top with remaining cheese. Refrigerate overnight. Bring to room temperature. Bake at 350° for 45 to 60 minutes. Check center for doneness with a toothpick.

Yield: 4 servings

Editors' Note: *The baked tomatoes (page 161) are an excellent side dish for this delicious breakfast or brunch casserole.*

Selected for *"Best Places to Stay Guides"*

―――――――――――

The original house burned and was rebuilt in 1840. The present 40-room mansion is the result of renovations and additions made in 1929 by U.S. Senator John S. Frelinghugsen of New Jersey who used the property as a hunting lodge.

The formal gardens (est. 1795) were restored and enhanced in the 1930's according to a design by noted landscape architect Loutrell Briggs.

Woodlands Resort & Inn

A 1906 Greek Revival mansion impeccably restored in the best English tradition.

Address: 125 Parsons Road
Summerville, SC 29483
Reservations: 1-800-774-9999
Telephone: (843) 875-2600
E-mail: reservations@woodlandsinn.com

Web Site: www.woodlandsinn.com
Category: Historic Inn
Proprietor: Marty Wall
Rates: $295-$395 (seasonal)

Woodlands Tea Scones with Berries and Sweet Cream

2 cups flour
½ teaspoon salt
1 tablespoon black pepper
½ stick butter
1 egg

½ cup milk
Egg wash
Sugar
1 pint crème fraîche (sweet cream)
Fresh seasonal berries

Sift dry ingredients and crumb in butter. Make a well in center of mixture and add beaten egg and milk. The dough must be sticky (add more milk, if needed). Scrape dough mixture into plastic wrap and pat out into a block. Refrigerate until cold, roll out (about 2-inch thick) on a floured surface, and cut into circles with a medium-sized biscuit cutter. Brush with egg wash and sprinkle with sugar before baking at 400° for 10 minutes. Serve with sweet cream and berries.

Yield: 12 scones

Editors' Notes: *We prefer adding 1 tablespoon of sugar to the scone mixture instead of the black pepper. If desired, scones may be dusted with powdered sugar after removing from oven instead of sprinkling with granulated before baking. The scones will be light brown on bottom, but they do not brown on top. Crème fraîche (krehm FRESH) can be pricey; however, you can create your own by combining 1 cup of whipping cream with 2 tablespoons of buttermilk in a glass container. Once mixed, cover and let stand at room temperature until very thick (8 to 24 hours).*

Croissant French Toast with Blueberries & Ice-Cream

1 (750 ml) bottle Elysium
½ cup sugar
1 tablespoon orange zest (peel)
1 cinnamon stick
1 cup fresh blueberries
4 eggs

½ cup cream
1 teaspoon vanilla extract
4 stale croissants, bottom & tops cut off
1 cup corn flakes, crushed
4 scoops of vanilla ice-cream

Pour Elysium (e-LEE-zi-um) into a pan and cook to burn off alcohol. To do this, pour wine in saucepan and simmer 2 to 3 minutes. Add next 3 ingredients and continue simmering until a syrup-like consistency is reached (mixture should coat back of a wooden spoon), about 10 to 15 minutes. Add berries and keep warm. After mixing next 3 ingredients together, soak croissant slices for 1 minute, turning over once. Dip each side of croissant slice into crushed corn flakes. Place on a greased cookie sheet and bake at 325° for 10 minutes. Place croissant slices on a plate and top with a scoop of ice-cream. Spoon berries over top of ice cream.

Yield: 4 servings

Editors' Notes: *Use frozen blueberries if fresh ones are not in season. Elysium is a California dessert wine available at a wine shop. If it cannot be found, substitute a sweet Port (such as a ruby Port) or another dessert wine. A 750 ml bottle equals approximately 3 cups. A recipe for a delicious and easy vanilla ice-cream is on page 164.*

"Outstanding--worth a special trip"
-- *Mobil Travel Guide*

"Among the top ten hotels for service in the world."
--*Conde Nast Traveler,* January 2002

"A 30-minute drive from Charleston, Woodlands is one of the finest places to stay in the Lowcountry." --*Frommer's Guide*

"The idea was to create a country house in the English tradition, but in the mood of the South."~ *Norman Gayle, Country Inns Magazine*

"Gracious without being overly grand, the Woodlands is the kind of civilized retreat that should be at the heart of any visit to town or country."
--*Town & Country Magazine, John Cantrell (March 2001)*

Oscar's

Quite simply fine dining at its best

Address: 207 W. 5th Street North
Summerville, SC 29483
Telephone: (843) 871-3800

Cuisine: American Eclectic
Executive Chef: David Langenstein
Price Range: Dinner/$8-$24

Bananas Oscar

1 ripe banana,
   sliced lengthwise and halved
4 tablespoons light rum
4 tablespoons banana liqueur
4 tablespoons brown sugar

3 tablespoon butter
4 scoops vanilla ice-cream
4 tablespoons candied pecans
Whipped cream, optional
Chopped pecans, optional

Peel and slice banana; set aside. Combine rum and next 3 ingredients in a sauté pan over medium heat. Bring to a simmer and add banana; cook briefly on each side. Keep warm.

Candied Pecans

4 ounces melted butter   2 cups pecan pieces   1 cup brown sugar

Combine all ingredients, spread evenly on a baking sheet, and bake at 450° for 8 to 10 minutes (do not overcook). Remove from oven and cool.

Assembly: Place 2 scoops of ice-cream in bowl with candied pecans and toss to coat. Place ice-cream in a bowl. Pour bananas and sauce over ice-cream. Garnish with whipped cream and more pecans, if desired.

Yield: 2 servings

Editors' Note: *Prepare candied pecans in advance and roll ice-cream scoops in cool pecans until covered. Place 2 scoops of pecan-covered ice-cream balls into individual banana split (or ice-cream) dishes and place in freezer until ready to use. Save extra candied pecans for making more ice-cream balls, topping green salads, or snacking.*

❧❧❧❧❧❧❧❧❧❧❧❧❧❧❧❧❧❧❧❧❧❧❧❧

Horseradish Encrusted Deep Fried Oysters Stuffed with Brie

½ cup freshly grated horseradish	Salt and pepper to taste
2 cups bread crumbs	Old Bay seasoning to taste
½ tablespoon fresh basil	18 large select oysters
1 tablespoon freshly chopped parsley	6 ounces Brie
½ cup milk	6 slices apple-smoked bacon
3 eggs, beaten	18 toothpicks
2 cups flour	2 cups mesclun greens for garnish

Heat oil in fryer to 350°. Mix horseradish and next 3 ingredients together until blended. Add milk to beaten eggs in a separate bowl. Season flour with salt, pepper, and Old Bay seasoning. Cut bacon strips into thirds. Cut a slit into side of each oyster; stuff with Brie, wrap with bacon, and skewer with a toothpick. Dredge stuffed oyster in flour, dip in egg mixture, and then coat with bread crumbs. Deep fry oysters until golden brown, removing toothpicks when done. Serve with Champagne Sauce and Onion Marmalade.

Yield: 6 servings

Editors' Notes: *Brie (BREE) is a popular French cheese that has a mellow, soft interior. If apple-smoked bacon is unavailable, substitute another smoked bacon. Mesclun (MEHS-kluhn) greens, also known as salad mix, is a combination of small, tender salad greens.*

Champagne Sauce

3 ounces champagne	6 ounces butter
1 teaspoon shallots	Parsley
1½ cups heavy cream	

Add champagne (sham-PAYN) and shallots to sauce pan; reduce by one-half. Add cream, reduce by one-half. Whip in butter. Garnish with parsley.

Onion Marmalade

1 jumbo onion (sliced)	2 tablespoons brown sugar
¼ cup apple cider vinegar	¼ cup dry sherry
2 tablespoons white sugar	Salt and pepper to taste

Heat heavy sauté pan. Add onion and cook until brown. Add next 4 ingredients and cook until dry. Add salt and pepper.

Considered "a restaurant worth repeating" among locals since 1982.

Seewee Restaurant

A general store turned into a restaurant serving homemade specialties

Address: 4808 Highway 17N
Awendaw, SC 29429
(north of Charleston)
Telephone: (843) 928-3609

Web Site: www.thefoodscoop.com/
seewee.html
Cuisine: Southern-style cooking & seafood
Price Range: Lunch/$5.95-$10.95
Dinner/$8.95-$19.95

Mary's Okra Soup

1 meaty ham bone
4 cups red ripe tomatoes, cored and chopped

4 cups fresh okra, cut cross-wise
Salt and pepper to taste

Place ham bone in 4 cups of boiling water. Lower heat and continue cooking until meat falls off bone. Add tomatoes (or purée) and cook for about an hour. Add okra last, season with salt and pepper, and cook on low heat until tender (about thirty minutes).

Yield: 6-8 servings

Contributor's Note: Four cups of tomato purée or 4 cups of canned tomatoes (undrained) may be substituted for fresh tomatoes. Two (6-ounce) packages of frozen okra may be substituted for fresh okra. For a good vegetable soup, add desired amount of fresh or frozen green lima beans and corn. Add beans with tomatoes and add corn with okra. Cook an additional hour.

Editors' Notes: *Instead of using a ham bone, brown 1 pound of ground chuck in a Dutch oven, breaking up with a metal spatula. Add 4 cups of water, tomatoes, okra, and season to taste. Before serving, sprinkle soup with grated Parmesan or Cheddar cheese. Extra good with additional vegetables (petite lima beans and shoepeg white corn) added. A dollop of sour cream, served on top, is also a tasty addition.*

Restaurants
Awendaw, South Carolina

Cowcountry Boil

3 pounds small white potatoes
Salt and pepper to taste
Old Bay seasoning, to taste
1 whole sliced lemon
3 garlic cloves

3 pounds Hillshire Sausage,
  cut in 1-inch slices
5 pound bag corn-on-the-cob,
  fresh or frozen
5 pounds shrimp, shells on
3 dozen small clams in shell

Put potatoes and seasonings in pot with enough water to cover; simmer until almost done. Add sausage and corn; cook until done. Add clams and shrimp; cook until pink. Serve hot.

Yield: 15 servings

Editors' Note: *Along the South Carolina/Georgia coast, a Lowcountry Boil is more than a popular meal, it is an event steeped in Lowcountry tradition. The classic coastal dish, sometimes referred to as Frogmore Stew, offers diners a variety of culinary choices in one big pot. It is served in a casual outdoor setting.*

Southern Collard Greens

1 meaty ham bone or salt pork
1 bunch (or bag) of fresh collard greens

1 teaspoon salt
Pepper, to taste

Thoroughly wash greens and strip leaves from stems. Break leaves into medium-sized pieces. Wash again and set aside. Place ham bone in a large pot, cover with water, and bring to a boil. Lower heat and continue low boil about 15 minutes. Add collard green, season with salt and pepper, cover. Cook on medium heat about 45 minutes or until tender (color will be a dark olive green). Remove meat and drain. Add more salt, if needed.

Yield: 4 servings

Editors' Notes: *Use only fresh collards. Frozen collards may be prepared using this recipe, but the flavor is not nearly as good. Serve with pepper vinegar sauce, sweet potatoes, and corn bread.*

Recommended by *1st Traveler's Choice.*

Recommended as one of the "top choices" for Lowcountry cuisine by travel writer Lynn Seldon, *New York Post.*

Listed as one of South Carolina's Secrets in
100 Secrets of the Carolina Coast,
by Randall H. Duckett and Maryellen K. Duckett

Trawler Seafood Restaurant

Its waterside location provides an authentic ambience in a relaxed setting.

Address: 100 Church Street
        Mt. Pleasant, SC 29464
Telephone: (843) 884-2560
Web Site: www.advantagecharleston.
        com/trawler

Cuisine: Specializing in seafood
Executive Chef: Michael Rogers
Price Range: Lunch/$5-$13
        Dinner/$13-$27

Crab Dip

1 pound crabmeat
1 tablespoon Worcestershire sauce
½ teaspoon Tabasco sauce
1 ounce chili sauce

2 ounces Cheddar cheese
½ teaspoon lemon juice
½ teaspoon prepared horseradish
½ cup mayonnaise (more if needed)

Mix all ingredients together; let sit for one hour to absorb flavors. Serve cold with crackers or toast points.

Yield: 8-10 servings

Editors' Note: *Make sure enough mayonnaise is added to enable crab to stick together when spreading.*

The Trawler Restaurant has been serving seafood to The Lowcountry for over 35 years.

Fruit de Mer
Lobster Stock

2 tablespoons olive oil
1¼ pounds lobster cavities, cut into 2-inch pieces
¼ cup yellow onion, diced
¼ cup celery, diced
¼ cup leek, white only, diced

¼ cup carrot, peeled and diced
1 teaspoon fresh parsley
¼ teaspoon fresh tarragon
1 bay leaf
1 whole black peppercorn
1 teaspoon white pepper

1 small tomato, seeded and diced
¼ small can tomato paste
½ cup brandy
3 quarts water

Heat olive oil in a stock pot. Add lobster cavities and sauté until bright red; add next 4 ingredients and sauté until soft. Stir in next 7 ingredients. Sauté mixture until thoroughly incorporated; deglaze with brandy. Slowly add water to stock pot and bring to a simmer. Cook for up to 1½ hours or until liquid has reduced by 25%. Strain liquid and put aside.

Lobster Sauce

4 tablespoons butter
¼ cup shallots, diced
¼ cup garlic, diced
½ cup all-purpose flour, sifted

¼ cup brandy
1 quarts lobster stock (above)
1 cup heavy cream (36% milk fat)
Salt & pepper, to taste

Melt butter in sauce pan and add first 2 ingredients; sauté until translucent. Slowly add flour to pan to create a roux. Add enough flour so that a spoon cleans bottom of pot. Cook roux, while stirring over low heat, until proper consistency and color are achieved. Deglaze with brandy. Slowly add cooled stock, stirring to prevent lumps from forming. Bring to a simmer to cook out taste of raw flour, then add heavy cream. Continue simmering to thicken and reduce sauce by one-fourth. Check seasoning to ensure proper flavor has been achieved. Use a strainer or sieve to strain liquid. Hold.

Fruit de Mer

1 teaspoon garlic, chopped fine
¼ cup leek (white only), thoroughly rinse grit from between leaves and slice

4 ounces shrimp
4 ounces scallops
2 ounces crab meat
1 tomato, peeled and diced

2 tablespoons basil, chopped
½ cup cream
1 pound linguine, cooked and drained

Begin sautéing first 2 ingredients in olive oil over moderate heat. When garlic and leek begin releasing an aroma, add seafood. Continue cooking and add ½ of tomato and basil. Shrimp and scallops should be cooked and tender. Add cream and lobster sauce (3 to 4 cups, depending on preference) and bring up to serving temperature. Put hot pasta on plates (or in bowls), ladle sauce and seafood over pasta top, garnish with remaining tomato (diced) and basil.

Yield: 4 servings

Editors' Notes: *Lobster stock is sometimes available in supermarkets and gourmet shops (or it can be ordered online at www.soupbases.com).*

Woodlands Dining Room

Woodland's Dining Room, the only AAA Five Diamond award-winning dining room in South Carolina, enjoys a stellar reputation from food critics around the world.

Address: 125 Parsons Road
            Summerville, SC 29483
Telephone: (843) 875-2600
Web Site: www.woodlandsinn.com/
            restaurant.htm
Cuisine: New American

Executive Chef: Ken Vedrinski
Price Range: $59 (A la carte menu)
            $120 ("Tasting" menu)
            $120 (Chef's Table in
                   the kitchen)

Butternut Squash Soup

3 strips smoked bacon
1 large sweet onion, chopped
3 stalks celery, peeled and chopped
1 large butternut squash, peeled, seeded,
     diced and cubed into 1-inch cubes
4 cups chicken stock (may use canned)

1 leek (white part only), chopped
1 cup crème fraîche (krehm FRESH)
     or whipping cream (see note on page 92)
Salt & white pepper, to taste
2 tablespoons of organic honey
Chives, pancetta, or smoked duck

Sauté first 3 ingredients, then add next 3 ingredients. Simmer until squash is soft; add next 4 ingredients and blend together. Pass through a strainer. Garnish with chives and pancetta or smoked duck.

Yield: 4-6 servings

Editors' Notes: *For ease in peeling squash, pierce it with a fork and then cook it in a microwave about 5 minutes (or until tender) as you would cook a baking potato. Peeled and cubed butternut squash is now available in the produce section of many grocery stores. Save the pulp of the squash, after straining, and place it in a casserole dish topped with bread crumbs. Bake at 350° for 30 minutes for a delicious side dish. A leek has a white stalk with a bulbous end, and it is related to both the onion and the garlic. According to legend, Nero thought a large consumption of leeks would improve his singing voice; he devoured them. Pancetta (pan-CHEH-tuh) is a salty, Italian bacon.*

Hot Smoked Maine Salmon

½ pound salt
½ pound sugar
1 tablespoon crushed black pepper

12 pieces of salmon
  (no bones, skin, or fat)
Applewood (for grilling)

Mix first 3 ingredients. Pack around salmon until completely covered and allow to sit at room temperature for 1 hour.

Marinade
1 cup apple cider
1 tablespoon fresh dill, chopped
1 teaspoon mustard seeds

Curry Oil
1 teaspoon curry powder
¼ cup grapeseed oil

Cook cider until reduced to syrup consistency; add dill and mustard seeds. Wash salt off salmon and cover with a thin layer of marinade. Combine grapeseed oil and curry powder; let sit for 3 hours. Light applewood over fire and grill salmon until a good burn develops. Put salmon in a 250° oven for 16 to 20 minutes. Let cool for 2 hours; pour curry oil around grilled salmon.

Yield: 12 servings

Editors' Notes: *Applewood is used for flavoring in the cooking process. Soak wood in water and place on top of heat source (grill or wood oven). Hickory or mesquite wood may be substituted for applewood, if using a wood-burning stove. The salmon may also be cooked on an electric griddle/grill or a charcoal-burning grill. Grapeseed oil, extracted from grape seeds, is usually imported from Europe. However, it can sometimes be found in gourmet shops. If unavailable, substitute canola or safflower oil.*

"The only perfect food score in North America."
-- Gold List/2002 *Reader's Choice Awards*

Conde Nast Traveler's 2000 Reader Poll named
The Dining Room at Woodlands
"one of the top three restaurants in North America."

A white-pillared Classical Revival building, originally constructed in 1906, Woodlands stands on 42 landscaped acres.

"The most beautiful city in North America" --*Le Monde*

❧❧❧❧❧❧❧❧❧❧❧❧❧❧❧❧❧❧❧❧

One of the "Top 12 Trendy Hot Spots in the World" --*New York Times*

❧❧❧❧❧❧❧❧❧❧❧❧❧❧❧❧❧❧❧❧

One of "America's Top 10 U. S. Cities to Visit" --*Conde Nast Traveler*

❧❧❧❧❧❧❧❧❧❧❧❧❧❧❧❧❧❧❧❧

One of "Top 200 places in the Country" --*Forbes Magazine*

❧❧❧❧❧❧❧❧❧❧❧❧❧❧❧❧❧❧❧❧

One of "Top 10 Southeast Cities for Family Vacations" --*Family Fun Magazine*

❧❧❧❧❧❧❧❧❧❧❧❧❧❧❧❧❧❧❧❧

"The stretch of coast from Savannah southward is...the most beautiful place in the world."   --Margaret Mitchell, author of *Gone With the Wind*

❧❧❧❧❧❧❧❧❧❧❧❧❧❧❧❧❧❧❧❧

Welcome to Savannah, the sultry and mysterious "Belle" of the Southeastern coast. Savannah captivates the suitors that come to call with her natural beauty, eccentric charm and traditional Southern Hospitality — because Savannah is genteel, gracious and captivating. Savannah is the beautifully preserved hidden treasure of the Low Country. Come unlock the history, romance and beauty that lies within. Explore every nook and cranny because you are her guest and Savannah loves sharing her treasures with you.

Web Site for Savannah, GA
www.savannahvisit.com

Savannah
"Soul of the South"

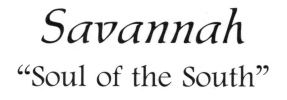

Original artwork by Theron Wallis

Picturesque Johnson Square is a magical place to savor Savannah

Ballastone Inn

Savannah's first and premiere Bed and Breakfast Inn

Address: 14 E. Oglethorpe Ave.
Savannah, GA 31401
(Historic District)
Reservations: 1-800-322-6603
Telephone: (912) 236-1484

Web Site: www.ballastone.com
Category: Historic Inn
Owners/Innkeepers:
Jim & Jennifer Sallandi
Rates: $195-$475 (seasonal)

Melon Breakfast Soup

1 ripe honey dew
1 ripe cantaloupe
¼ cup orange juice
2 ripe bananas

2 tablespoons lemon juice
½ cup whipped cream or plain yogurt
2 tablespoons fresh or dry dill
Sliced strawberries or a fresh mint sprig

In a food processor, purée melons 2 cups at a time, adding a little orange juice to assist in purée process. Purée melons until smooth and lump free. Pour into a large bowl. Next, purée bananas, adding lemon juice to prevent browning. Add puréed bananas to melon mixture. Then add the dill and whipped cream (or plain yogurt) to melon and banana mixture. Gently whip together and chill two hours or overnight. Garnish with sliced strawberries or a fresh mint sprig, if desired.

Yield: 6 servings

Editors' Notes: *If purchasing pre-cut melon chunks, use about 2 cups of honey dew and 2 cups of cantaloupe. We prefer this recipe prepared with whipped cream, rather than yogurt; the taste seems richer and the consistency appears creamier. This is an ideal breakfast or luncheon soup during the warmer months.*

᦯᦯᦯᦯᦯᦯᦯᦯᦯᦯᦯᦯᦯᦯᦯᦯᦯᦯᦯᦯᦯᦯᦯

Sweet Rolls

½ cup water	¼ cup warm water	½ cup light brown sugar
½ cup milk	½ teaspoon sugar	1 tablespoon cinnamon
3 tablespoons butter	1 tablespoon yeast	1 cup pecans, optional
1 teaspoon salt	1 egg	½ cup raisins, optional
2 tablespoons sugar	1 cup butter or margarine,	
4-5 cups all-purpose flour	room temperature	

Combine first 5 ingredients in a saucepan. Heat mixture until butter is melted. Set aside to cool. Pour 4 cups of flour into a large bowl or mixer bowl; make a well in center and set aside. In a small mixing bowl, combine next 3 ingredients and allow mixture to rise (about 5 minutes). After first mixture has cooled, add egg. Combine two mixtures. Stir and pour into flour well. Using dough hook of a mixer, mix until smooth and elastic. Remove dough from bowl. If dough is very sticky, add more flour until dough is soft and manageable. Knead dough by hand for an additional 3 to 5 minutes or until dough is smooth. Put dough into a well greased bowl and cover with plastic. Allow to double in size (35 minutes to 1 hour). While dough is rising, whip together next 3 ingredients. Set aside. Once dough has doubled in size, beat down and divide into two equal pieces. Roll out one piece at a time and spread with butter mixture. Once dough is completely covered, sprinkle with nuts and/or raisins. Begin rolling dough from top to bottom, pulling the dough as it is being rolled. Once the dough is completely rolled, cut each log into 2-inch round pieces and place into greased pans. Repeat with remaining dough. Cover each pan with plastic and allow dough to double in size (about 30 minutes). Once doubled, unwrap and bake in a 350° oven 25 to 30 minutes or until golden brown. Allow to cool slightly, and then pour or drizzle icing over top of rolls.

Yield: 12 rolls

Icing

1 (1-pound) box powdered (10-X) sugar   ¼ cup half-and-half (or milk)

Mix together until smooth. Add more milk, if needed.

Editors' Note: *Our friend who tested this recipe, one of the best home-bakers we know, reports: "It is the best sweet roll recipe I've ever used." Instead of using the dough hooks of a mixer, she kneaded the dough (by hand) for 9 minutes. She recommends putting all the rolls into a 9 x 13-inch pan, sprayed with a non-stick spray, for the second rise and baking time.*

"Best In the State" --Zagat Survey 2001

"Savannah is Georgian elegance ... a state of grace encouraged at The Ballastone Inn."
--*Condé Nast Traveler*

"It is worth the effort to obtain such accommodations if you really want to walk
in Savannah's spirit." --*The New York Times*

Eliza Thompson House

Southern hospitality and romantic elegance for discriminating travelers

Address: 5 West Jones Street
Savannah, GA 31401
(Historic District)
Reservations: 1-800-348-9378
Telephone: (912) 236-3620

Web Site: www.elizathompsonhouse.com
Category: Historic Inn
Innkeeper: Jean Bearden
Rates: $169-$269 (seasonal)

Miss Virginia's Peach and Pecan Dip

8 ounces cream cheese   4 ounces peach preserves   1 cup chopped pecans

Bring the cream cheese to room temperature and blend in a small food processor (or with a hand beater) until smooth. Stir in peach preserves and mix well. Fold in chopped pecans, reserving a teaspoonful to sprinkle on top. Refrigerate for at least 2 hours before serving. Serve chilled or at room temperature with your favorite crackers or toasted bread rounds.

Yield: 10-12 servings

Editors' Notes: *Another flavor of preserves, such as apricot or strawberry, may be substituted for the peach. This dip also makes a nice topping for small open-faced sandwiches on a party tray.*

Salsa Egg Casserole

⅛ cup mild salsa
⅛ cup shredded Cheddar cheese
3 eggs

1 ounce chopped green chilies
¾ cup milk

Preheat oven to 350°. Grease a 9 X 13-inch glass baking dish. Spread salsa on bottom of dish. Sprinkle cheddar cheese evenly over the salsa. Mix together the next 3 ingredients and pour mixture over cheese. Bake at 350° for 40 to 50 minutes, or until eggs are firm.

Yield: 4 servings

The Eliza Thompson House, a Federal style three-story mansion is one of the oldest bed and breakfast inns in Savannah. Built for Eliza Thompson in 1847, the landmark recalls a prosperous time in Savannah where elegant parties in fine homes were popular.

The Foley House Inn

A unique combination of Southern hospitality and European charm

Address: 14 W. Hull Street
Savannah, GA 31401
(Historic District)
Reservations: 1~800~647~3708
Telephone: (912) 232~6622

Web Site: www.foleyinn.com
Category: Historic Inn
Owners/Innkeepers:
Beryl & Donald Zerwer
Rates: $200~$345 (seasonal)

Collard Green Soufflé

1 cup cooked collard greens, drained
6 eggs

½ cup heavy cream
Salt, pepper, & chives, to taste

Place 1 tablespoon of cooked collard greens in bottom of 6 individual ramekin cups (sprayed with baking spray or wiped with butter). Beat eggs and stir in remaining ingredients; pour mixture over the "greens." Microwave on high for 2 to 3 minutes until soufflé (soo-FLAY) is puffed. Serve with a sprinkling of chives and/or paprika.

Yield: 6 servings

Editors' Notes: *Frozen collards may be used, if desired. This breakfast dish is good topped with grated Cheddar cheese (add before microwaving). Chopped spinach, seasoned with salt and pepper, may be substituted for the collard greens.*

❧❧❧❧❧❧❧❧❧❧❧❧❧❧❧❧❧❧❧❧❧❧❧❧❧❧

Cheese Blintzes
Batter

1 cup milk	4 eggs	Pinch salt
1 cup flour	¼ cup sugar	Butter-flavored
1 tablespoon sour cream	1 teaspoon vanilla	cooking spray

Combine first 3 ingredients, blending well. Mix in 1 egg at a time, using a hand-beater, until batter is smooth. Stir in next 3 ingredients. Heat a crêpe (KRAYP) or 6-inch frying pan over high heat until very hot, but not smoking. Spray bottom of pan with cooking spray or wipe with a piece of slightly buttered waxed paper; return to lowered heat. Cover bottom of pan with thin layer of batter, turning in all directions until batter covers entire bottom of pan. Pour out any excess (crêpes should be ultra-thin). Cook until golden on one side, approximately 1 minute, and then turn and cook until golden on other side. When cooked, remove crêpe and stack on a platter. Repeat until all batter is used, re-greasing pan between crêpes. Makes 6-8 crêpes, depending on size of pan.

Filling

1 cup cottage cheese	1 egg yolks	½ teaspoon vanilla
4 ounces cream cheese	3 teaspoons sugar	

Mix all ingredients for the filling and set aside.

Coulis

½ cup cherries (pitted), blueberries, or raspberries	¼ cup sugar	1 tablespoons cornstarch, dissolved in water
½ cup water	½ teaspoon lemon juice	

Boil fruit and water for 3 minutes. Over medium heat, stirring constantly, add sugar and lemon juice. Bring mixture back to a boil and slowly stir in the dissolved cornstarch mixture. Boil coulis (kool-LEE) 1 minute to thicken.

Assembly

Fill each crêpe with approximately 3 tablespoons of filling. Fold outsides to center and roll blintze (BLIHNTS) until completely closed. Place rolled blintzes in a pan and sauté about 2 minutes, turning once. When ready to serve, place blintzes in a 350° oven for about 20 minutes. Ladle coulis over blintzes after transferring to serving platter or individual plates.

Yield: 6 servings

Editors' Notes: *If possible, prepare crêpes in advance--especially if serving this dish to guests. The crêpes may be frozen stacked; they may be filled before freezing or after defrosting. Preparing crêpes in advance is a tremendous time-saver and highly recommended.*

Named By *Discovering Traveler*
as a Top "Romantic Hideaway of 1999"

Rated one of ten "Most Romantic Inns" in the country
by *Vacation Magazine.*

Forsyth Park Inn

*Built in circa 1890, this Queen Anne Victorian mansion
overlooks Savannah's largest and most opulent park*

Address: 102 W. Hall Street
Savannah, GA 31401
(Historic District)
Reservations: 1-800-484-6850
Telephone: (912) 233-6800

Web Site: www.forsythparkinn.com
Category: Historic Inn
Owners/Innkeepers: Lori & Richard Blass
Rates: $115-$230 (seasonal)

Fresh Fruit with Honey Yogurt Dip

2 cups vanilla yogurt
½ cup honey
1 teaspoon ground cinnamon

Assorted fresh fruit
(apples, bananas, pineapple, strawberries, etc.)
cut into wedges or bite-size pieces

Combine first 3 ingredients in a small bowl; stir to blend. Place bowl on platter. Surround with fresh fruit and serve.

Yield: 2 cups

Editors' Note: *A refreshing dip anytime, especially when fresh fruits are in season.*

Bed & Breakfasts and Historic Inns
Savannah, Georgia

୬ଔ୬ଔ୬ଔ୬ଔ୬ଔ୬ଔ୬ଔ୬ଔ୬ଔ୬ଔ୬ଔ୬ଔ୬ଔ୬ଔ

Best-Ever Orange Sponge Cake

6 egg whites	6 egg yoks
1¾ cup sifted all-purpose flour, divided	6 tablespoons fresh orange juice
¼ teaspoon salt	1 tablespoon freshly grated orange peel
1½ cups granulated sugar	10-X powdered sugar

In large bowl of electric mixer, let egg whites warm to room temperature (about 1 hour). Sift about 2 cups of flour onto a sheet of waxed paper; fill cups to slightly overflowing and level with spatula to make 1¾ level cups. Sift flour again with salt. Set aside. With electric mixer at medium speed, beat egg whites until foamy. Gradually beat in ½ cup of the granulated sugar, 2 tablespoons at a time, beating well after each addition. Continue beating until stiff peaks form when beaters are slowly raised. Set aside. Preheat oven to 350°

In small bowl of electric mixer, with the same beaters at high speed, beat egg yolks until thick and lemon-colored (about 3 minutes). Do not underbeat. Gradually beat in remaining 1 cup granulated sugar, and continue beating until mixture is smooth. At low speed, blend flour mixture and orange juice, alternately, into egg yolk mixture; begin and end with flour, guiding batter into beaters with scraper. Add orange peel. With a whisk or rubber spatula, using an under-and-over motion, fold yolk mixture gently into whites.

Pour batter into an ungreased 9¾-10 x 4½-inch kugelhopf or tube pan (one without a removable bottom). Bake 50 to 55 minutes in kugelhopf or 35 to 40 minutes in tube pan, until cake springs back when pressed with finger. Invert over a bottle. If using tube pan, invert cake onto a plate. Cool completely. Using an up-and-down motion, run spatula around the edge of cake and tube. Invert cake and shake to release. Place on serving plate or cake stand. Sprinkle powdered sugar over top of cake. To cut cake, use a knife with serrated edge. Cut gently, going back and forth with sawing motion.

Yield: 1 cake

Editors' Notes: *A kugelhopf (KOO-guhl-hopf) pan is turbular-shaped, tube mold with swirled sides. They can be found in gourmet or kitchenware shops. A Bundt (BUHNT) pan may be substituted. Make a Lemon Sponge Cake by substituting fresh lemon juice and lemon peel for the orange juice and orange peel.*

An elegant mansion restored to create the pampered lifestyle of the nineteenth century.

The Gastonian

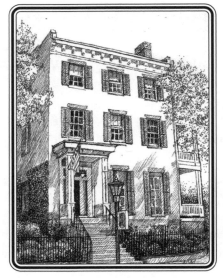

*The only Relais & Chateaux property in Georgia, The Gastonian
is known all over the world for its legendary hospitality and historic elegance.*

Address: 220 E. Gaston Street
Savannah, GA 31401
(Historic District)
Reservations: 1-800-322-6603
Telephone: (912) 232-2869

Web Site: www.gastonian.com
Category: Historic Inn
Owner/Innkeeper: Anne Landers
Rates: $250-$425 (seasonal)

Lemon Ricotta Cheese Pancakes

1 cup all-purpose flour
3 tablespoons sugar
4 teaspoons baking powder
½ teaspoon salt

6 teaspoons lemon juice
2 cups part skim milk ricotta cheese
6 eggs, separated
¼ cup corn oil

Combine first 4 ingredients in bowl of an electric mixer. Beat in next 2 ingredients until smooth. Beat egg whites until stiff peaks form; set aside. Beat eggs yolks and oil into flour mixture. Fold eggs whites into batter after all ingredients are combined. Stir until smooth. Heat a lightly greased griddle (or skillet) over medium-high heat. Ladle batter onto griddle to form 3-inch cakes. Cook until small bubbles form and the edges begin browning, 2 to 3 minutes. Turn cakes and continue cooking 1 to 2 minutes longer, until just cooked through. Repeat procedure until all batter is used.

Yield: 12 pancakes

Editors' Notes: *Light and delicious, these pancakes are ideal to serve on a spring morning. We think the addition of 2 teaspoons of lemon zest enhances the wonderful flavor even more. Garnish with powdered sugar and serve with syrup, if desired.*

꩜꩜꩜꩜꩜꩜꩜꩜꩜꩜꩜꩜꩜꩜꩜꩜꩜꩜꩜꩜꩜꩜꩜꩜

Vidalia Onion Bites

1 cup mayonnaise
1 cup Parmesan cheese
1 Vidalia onion, finely chopped

Sliced bread, crust removed
(white or wheat works best)

Mix all ingredients and spread onto bread. Cut into bite-size pieces and bake at 375° for approximately 10 minutes or until light brown.

Yield: About 3 dozen servings

Editors' Note: *An easy and delicious hors d'oeuvre using Georgia's famous Vidalia onions. If Vidalia onions are unavailable, use another sweet onion.*

Ham Bites

1 cup fine, dry breadcrumbs, divided
1 cup ground cooked ham
2 eggs, beaten
½ cup shredded sharp Cheddar cheese

¼ cup grated onion
2 tablespoons brown sugar
1 tablespoon Dijon mustard
Parsley

Combine ½ cup of bread crumbs with remaining ingredients in a large bowl. Stir well. Shape ham mixture into 1-inch balls and roll into remaining ½ cup bread crumbs, pressing firmly so crumbs adhere. Cover and chill for 30 minutes. Next place ham bites onto a lightly greased baking sheet and bake for 10 to 20 minutes at 360°. You may also deep-fry these bites for 2 minutes in vegetable oil, if desired. Garnish with parsley.

Yield: 2½ dozen

Editors' Notes: *For an extra crunchy coating, we use panko bread crumbs mixed in with seasoned bread crumbs (packaged). This is a delicious recipe, and the ham mixture may be formed into 3-inch patties to serve with Southern grits (page 30) or an egg dish. These ham balls may be frozen until time to bake.*

"...one of the best inns in the United States."   *--The Andrew Harper Report*

"...the Grand Dame of Savannah inns." *--Great Country Inns*

"...The most famous of Savannah inns and justifiably so."
-- The New York Times

"...one of the 12 most romantic inns on the East Coast." *---The Discerning Traveler*

Featured in February 2002 edition of *Architectural Digest.*

Granite Steps

An inn with a subtle difference of elegance

Address: 126 E. Gaston Street
Savannah, GA 31401
(Historic District)
Telephone: (912) 233-5380

Web Site: www.granitesteps.com
Category: Historic Inn
Owner/Innkeeper: Donna Sparks
Rates: $250-$500 (seasonal)

Berry Good French Toast Bake

½ cup flour
1½ cups milk
2 tablespoons sugar
½ teaspoon vanilla
¼ teaspoon salt
1 teaspoon cinnamon
½ teaspoon nutmeg
6 eggs

10 slices (1-inch thick) French bread,
    cut into 1 inch cubes
3-ounces cream cheese,
    cut into ½-inch cubes (see note below)
1 cup fresh or frozen blueberries
½ cup chopped pecans
Melted butter, enough to drizzle top
Powdered sugar, for garnishing

Generously grease a 1 x 3 x 9-inch pan or baking dish. Beat first 8 ingredients in a large bowl with hand beater until smooth. Stir in bread cubes until coated. Pour bread mixture into pan, topping evenly with next 3 ingredients. Cover and refrigerate up to 24 hours. Heat oven to 400°. Uncover dish and bake 20 to 25 minutes, or until golden brown. Drizzle with melted butter and sprinkle with powdered sugar. Serve with syrup, if desired.

Yield: 8 servings

Editors' Notes: *The cubes of cream cheese tend to maintain their shape, instead of melting, during cooking process. We suggest spreading an 8-ounce block of softened cream cheese on top over bread mixture and then sprinkling with sugar-sprinkled blueberries. If possible, let casserole come to room temperature before baking or else bake 5 to 10 minutes longer for cream cheese to melt.*

❧❧❧❧❧❧❧❧❧❧❧❧❧❧❧❧❧❧❧❧❧❧❧❧❧❧❧

Artichoke Dip

1 (16-ounce) can artichoke hearts, drained	Tabasco sauce to taste
1 cup mayonnaise	1 cup grated Parmesan cheese
1 tablespoon lemon juice	1 bag tortilla chips

Preheat oven to 350°. Place artichokes in bowl of food processor and process until roughly chopped. Add remaining ingredients and mix well. Bake for 10 minutes or until bubbly. Serve with tortilla chips.

Yield: 6 servings

Editors' Notes: *Just as good when reheated. We also like this dip served on Triscuits.*

The Granite Steps Baked Brie

1 (14-ounce) round of Brie	¼ cup brown sugar
1 can Pillsbury crescent rolls	Raspberries or other fresh fruit

Preheat oven to 350°. Unroll crescent rolls; instead of pulling apart perforations into triangles, divide into two squares. Place one square on bottom of Brie (BREE), top Brie with brown sugar, and then top with other crescent square. Pinch edges together around the Brie. Place wrapped Brie on a foil covered cookie sheet and bake until golden brown. Top with fresh fruit and serve with crackers.

Yield: 12 servings

Editors' Notes: *For a crunchy taste, sprinkle ¼ cup sliced, toasted almonds over brown sugar before adding pastry topping. Brush top of dough with an egg wash for a glossy appearance. Scumptious when topped with raspberries or other fresh fruit. Serve with Nabisco Social Tea crackers or crackers of your choice. To make Brie less sweet, use an herbed Brie and serve with a more salty cracker or water wafers.*

Voted Savannah's #1 Inn by *TravelHost* Magazine.
September 2001

*Selected as a site for a scene in Clint Eastwood's film version
of the New York Times best seller
Midnight in the Garden of Good and Evil.*

Hamilton Turner Inn

Savannah's "Grand Victorian Lady"

Address: 330 Abercorn Street
Savannah, GA 31401
(Historic District)
Reservations: 1-888-448-8849
Telephone: (912) 233-1833

E-mail: info@hamilton-turnerinn.com
Web Site: www.hamilton-turnerinn.com
Category: Historic Inn
Owners/Innkeepers: Jane & Rob Sales
Rates: $175-$295 (seasonal)

Benjamin's Baked Pancake

3 eggs
1 cup flour
1 teaspoon cinnamon
1 teaspoon nutmeg

2 tablespoons sugar
1 teaspoon vanilla
1½ cups milk
3 tablespoons butter

Preheat oven to 375-400°. Combine first 7 ingredients. Mix well. Melt butter until bubbly (but not brown) and pour into a deep-dish pie pan or a square casserole dish. Quickly pour all batter into pan and put into preheated oven. Bake for 20 to 30 minutes or until golden brown and firm. The sides will be high and dry; center will be shallow and soft. Slip pancake onto plate and fill center with fruit and/or sour cream, jam, or sprinkle with 10-X sugar and a squeeze of lemon.

Yield: 4 servings

Editors' Notes: *This is a versatile dish which lends itself to a variety of delicious variations. We especially like the dish sprinkled with 10-X sugar, topped with a dollop of sour cream, and finished off with strawberries sprinkled with more 10-X sugar. It is also excellent sprinkled with 10-X sugar and lemon juice. If uncertain which filling to use, serve it plain and provide an assortment of toppings so each person may make their own selection.*

❧❧❧❧❧❧❧❧❧❧❧❧❧❧❧❧❧❧❧❧❧❧❧

Ben's Barbeque Honey Soy Shrimp

Juice of 1 large lemon
2 tablespoons olive oil
1 tablespoon soy sauce
1 tablespoon honey
½ tablespoon Cajun seasoning
1 teaspoon ground red pepper

1 teaspoon fresh garlic
1 tablespoon fresh parsley,
  chopped and divided
1 pound medium shrimp,
  peeled and deveined
1 tablespoon grated lemon zest

Combine first 7 ingredients plus ½ tablespoon of the parsley. Let shrimp marinate in mixture at least one hour. Either barbeque marinated shrimp on moderately hot coals or broil in oven until lightly browned. After shrimp has cooked, sprinkle with lemon zest and remaining parsley. Serve over toasted sliced French bread (for an appetizer) or over rice to use as a main dish.

Yield: 4 appetizer servings or 2 main dish servings

Editors' Note: *For a less spicy taste, reduce amount of Cajun seasoning and red pepper.*

Ozella's Famous Shortbread

2 sticks real butter, softened
¾ cup sugar

2 cups self-rising flour
Powdered 10-X sugar

Cream butter and sugar, in a mixing bowl of a stand-up mixer, on medium-low speed until fluffy. Add flour and mix thoroughly. Stop once, scrape sides, and mix again. Roll or spread batter out (about ½-inch thick) onto a greased or parchment-lined cookie sheet. Bake in 325° oven for 30 minutes or until lightly browned. Sprinkle with powdered sugar and cut into small squares.

Yield: Approximately 30 pieces of shortbread

Editors' Notes: *This 3-ingredient recipe seems too easy to be so good. Margarine or a "light" butter will not work in this recipe. Real butter is needed to produce the rich, buttery flavor that makes it so tasty. Also, be sure not to substitute regular flour for self-rising flour. Wonderful served with afternoon tea. Keep shortbread stored in an airtight container and extra batter on-hand in freezer.*

*Built in 1873 for a wealthy jeweler,
the Hamilton-Turner House represents one of the finest examples
of the Second French Empire styles of architecture in the United States.*

Magnolia Place

One of Savannah's grand inns

Address: 503 Whitaker Street
Savannah, GA 31401
(Historic District)
Reservations: 1-800-238-7674
Telephone: (912) 236-7674

E-mail: info@magnoliaplaceinn.com
Web Site: www.magnoliaplaceinn.com
Category: Historic Inn
Owners/Innkeepers: Connie & Steve Fobes
Rates: $150-$295 (seasonal)

Anna K's Pistachio Biscotti

¾ teaspoon almond extract
3 teaspooons vanilla
¾ cup olive oil
3 eggs

2¼ cups flour
1½ cups sugar
2¼ cups pistachios
¾ cup dried cranberries

Preheat oven to 350°. Combine all liquids, except eggs. Next, add eggs. After combining dry ingredients, stir in wet ingredients. Mix in pistachios and cranberries with moistened hands. Divide dough in half and place 2 logs on a parchment or wax paper-lined cookie sheet. Bake 35 minutes or until dough is light brown. Reduce temperature in oven to 275° and then remove biscotti from oven. After cooling for 10 minutes, cut biscotti into diagonal or rectangular portions, ¾-inch thick. Place cooled biscotti back on lined cookie sheet; return to oven for 8 to 10 minutes to dry out. Cool and store in an air tight container.

Yield: Approximately 3 dozen pieces

Editors' Notes: *Biscotti (bee-SKAWT-tee) is a crunchy, twice-baked Italian biscuit/cookie. This biscotti recipe is as good as any I (Maxine) have had in Italy, and it is so easy to prepare! Pistachios (pih-STASH-ee-ohs) are now available already shelled, and the dough can be frozen until ready to use. Indescribably good dipped into coffee or a dessert wine.*

Bed & Breakfasts and Historic Inns
Savannah, Georgia

Anna's Praline French Toast

8 eggs
½ cup half-and-half
6 pieces white sandwich bread
1 stick butter

½ cup brown sugar
⅔ cup maple syrup
2 cups chopped pecans

Mix first two ingredients together. Place bread slices in a greased dish and cover with egg mixture. Refrigerate overnight. The next day, melt butter in a saucepan. Add sugar and syrup; stir in chopped pecans. Pour pecan mixture over the bread and bake at 350° 50 t0 60 minutes. The pecan topping should be set with the bread still soft and fluffy.

Yield: 6 servings

Editors' Note: *An easy-to-prepare, make-ahead dish that everyone raves over. It tastes even better if allowed to sit for 10 to 15 minutes after coming out of oven. This dish reheats well.*

Miss Ozzie's Chicken Salad

4 deboned, skinless chicken breasts
Lawry's seasoned salt, to taste
Garlic pepper, to taste
2 stalks of celery, chopped

5 or 6 green onions, chopped
3 tablespoons fresh parsely, chopped
½ cup mayonnaise

Season both sides of chicken breasts with salt and pepper; bake in 350° oven (or microwave) until juice runs clear and chicken is no longer pink. Allow chicken to cool before chopping into bite-sized pieces. While waiting for chicken to cool, combine next 3 ingredients. Add cooled chicken mixture. Next, add mayonnaise, a little at a time, until desired consistency is reached; it is important that the mayonnaise not be added all at one time. Taste and adjust seasoning with more salt and pepper, if desired.

Yield: 4 servings

Editors' Notes: *Be sure to use Lawry's seasoned salt--it is the secret ingredient. This delicious chicken salad is also good with chopped pecans added. If serving on bread or as small finger sandwiches, be careful not to use too much mayonnaise or bread will become soggy. The recipe may be prepared up to 24 hours in advance to allow time for flavors to blend.*

"Magnolia Place, an 1878 structure overlooking the verdant sprawl of Forsyth Park...
one of the mansions that arose around the Victorian park,
Magnolia Place was four years under construction." ---*Southern Living*

"Magnolia Place, with its pale yellow clapboard exterior,
has the look of a dignified old house... Inside, the inn is filled with English antiques,
period prints, and porcelains from around the world."
---*Luxury Inns & Resorts of the World*

The Presidents' Quarters

An inn of distinction harboring Savannah history—a place in time where diplomats, generals, and governors planned and influenced Savannah's history.

Address: 225 E. President Street
Savannah, Georgia 31401
(Historic District)
Reservations: 1-800-233-1776
Telephone: (912) 233-1600

Web Site: www.presidentsquarters.com
Category: Historic Inn
Owners: Raymond Clawson
Rhonda Mills
Rates: $137-$250 (Seasonal)

Crabby Mushroom Caps

1 (4-ounce) package cream cheese
½ pound crab meat
1 tablespoon mayonnaise
Pinch of dill

Dash of liquid smoke
1 pound fresh mushrooms
Melted butter
Parsley or chives

Soften cream cheese; combine next four ingredients. Remove stems from mushroom caps and, if needed, wipe caps with damp paper towel (never wash fresh mushrooms). Brush caps with a light coating of melted butter. Fill caps with crab mixture. Bake for 15 minutes at 375°. Garnish with parsley or chives.

Yield: Fills approximately 24 mushroom caps

Editors' Note: *This mixture is also excellent served chilled as a spread on crackers.*

๛๛๛๛๛๛๛๛๛๛๛๛๛๛๛๛๛๛๛๛๛

Apple Krispin' Bread

1 egg
½ cup corn oil
½ cup milk
1 cup sugar
1 teaspoon vanilla
2½ cups sifted white flour

1 teaspoon baking soda
½ teaspoon baking powder
¼ teaspoon salt
2 cups diced Granny Smith apples

Topping

1 cup brown sugar
2 tablespoons flour
1 teaspoon cinnamon

⅓ cup chopped nuts
   (walnuts, hazelnuts, or pecans)

Preheat oven to 350°. Beat together first 5 ingredients. Add next five ingredients and mix, lightly, until lumpy. Mix topping in separate bowl. Pour mixture into a prepared loaf pan (buttered, oiled, or sprayed with baking spray) and crumble 2-3 tablespoons of topping over dough. Bake for 45 minutes or until top is firm (check the middle, with a toothpick, for doneness). To moisten bread, freeze overnight before eating.

Yield: 15-20 servings

Editors' Note: *Granny Smith apples have freckled green skin and are slightly tart (we hope this isn't descriptive of Granny Smith, whoever she is!).*

"Gracious living indeed!
And the staff is genuinely friendly and interested."
-- Terry Houston, *The London Herald*

"When you go back and stay a fourth or fifth time, it's like staying in a friend's house. They value the relationship they have with you."
-- JoBeth McDaniel, *Working Women*

Located on Oglethorpe Square, these twin Federal style townhouses were built in 1855 under the auspices of the W. W. Gordon (grandfather of Juliette Gordon Lowe) Estate. It is across the street from The Owens-Thomas house, famous for its Regency architecture and the balcony from which Marquis de Lafayette once presented a speech during a visit to Savannah.

The Stephen Williams House

A stellar example of a 19th century Federal-style house

Address: 128 W. Liberty Street
Savannah, GA 31401
(Historic District)
Telephone: (912) 495-0032

Web Site: www.thestephenwilliamshouse.com
Category: B&B
Owner/Innkeeper: Albert Wall
Rates: $145-$325 (seasonal)

Stephen Williams House Breakfast Casserole

1 pound bulk sausage
4 slices white bread
1 medium onion, finely minced
1 (8-ounce) can mushrooms, drained
1 cup Cheddar or Swiss cheese
6 eggs

2 cups milk
1 teaspoon Worcestershire sauce
1 dash Tabasco sauce
¾ teaspoon salt
½ teaspoon pepper
¼ cup fresh Parmesan cheese, grated

Preheat oven to 350°. Brown sausage; chop finely and drain. Break up bread and put into buttered 13 x 9 x 2-inch baking dish. Sauté onion. Spoon sausage evenly over bread, onion over sausage, and mushrooms over onion. Sprinkle with Cheddar or Swiss cheese. Beat together next six ingredients and pour over mixture in baking dish. Just before baking, sprinkle with Parmesan cheese. Bake 35 to 40 minutes.

Yield: 6-8 servings

Editors' Notes: *Can be prepared the night before and refrigerated. Serving in individual ramekins makes a nice presentation. Canned (grated) Parmesan cheese may be substituted if fresh Parmesan is unavailable. Garnish with fresh rosemary.*

Bed & Breakfasts and Historic Inns
Savannah, Georgia

Madeira Wine Jelly

4 cups Madeira wine
6 cups sugar

6 ounces liquid Certo
Paraffin

Mix first two ingredients in top of a large double boiler (or a heavy pot). Place over boiling water and stir until mixture comes to a rolling boil; remove from heat and stir in Certo. Skim foam, if there is any. Pour mixture into hot, sterilized 8-ounce jelly jars and cover with ⅛–inch hot paraffin.

Yield: 8-10 half pints

Editors' Notes: *Madeira (muh-DEER-uh) wine is a Portuguese wine which can be very sweet or quite dry. Certo is an ingredient which aids in gelling process of jelly; Ball fruit jell liquid pectin may be substituted, if desired. If you have a canner, which seals the jelly, paraffin is not necessary. After pouring mixture into jars, center the heated jar lids on jars and screw band down evenly and firmly. Process filled jars in a water bath canner for 10 to 15 minutes. This jelly is a lovely color and delicious served with croissants.*

Imperial Crab Spread

¼ cup Hellmann's mayonnaise
2 teaspoons lemon juice
1 tablespoon small capers
½ teaspoon Worcestershire sauce

Dash of Tabasco sauce
1 pound fresh lump crabmeat
Bremner wafers or Carr's crackers

Mix first five ingredients in a medium bowl; gently toss in crabmeat. Taste before serving; the flavor may be enhanced by adding a little more lemon juice. Serve cold with wafers or crackers.

Yield: 12 servings

Featured in *The Atlanta Journal & Constitution's* Home and Garden section
(April 17, 2003)

Featured on Savannah's 2003 Spring Tour of Homes and Gardens, the newly restored Stephen Williams House is posed to become one of Savannah's pre-eminent bed and breakfast inns.

William Kehoe House

A stately Renaissance Revival mansion overlooking Columbia Square

Address: 123 Habersham Street
Savannah, GA 31401
(Historic District)
Reservations: 1-800-820-1020
Telephone: (912) 232-1020

Web Site: www.williamkehoehouse.com
Category: Historic Inn
Owners: Bonnie & Tom Sawyer
Rates: $205-$295 (seasonal)

Chocolate Chip Praline Pecan Pie

3 eggs
½ cup sugar
¼ cup cornstarch, sifted
2 ounces praline liqueur

1 cup chopped pecans
1 cup chocolate chips
4 ounces melted butter
1 (9-inch) unbaked pie shell

Preheat oven to 350°. Add all ingredients together and mix well. Pour into the unbaked pie shell and bake for 50 to 60 minutes. Filling may appear to be undercooked, but it will not be. Do not refrigerate.

Yield: 6-8 servings

Editors' Notes: *Walnuts may be substituted for pecans, if desired. Good topped with whipped cream flavored with more praline (PRAY-leen) liqueur.*

Sweet Potato Pecan Pancakes

1½ cups white flour
½ cup wheat flour
2 teaspoons baking powder
½ teaspoon baking soda
1 teaspoon cinnamon
¼ teaspoon ginger
½ cup chopped pecans
3 eggs

1 tablespoon orange zest (grated rind)
2 cups buttermilk
2½ cups canola oil
1¾ cups peeled, boiled, mashed sweet
   potato (may use canned)
2 tablespoons brown sugar
1 teaspoon vanilla

In large bowl stir together first 7 ingredients. In a separate bowl combine remaining ingredients. Add to dry ingredients and stir just until well-mixed. Pour batter onto a hot griddle in portions of approximately one-third cup; it may need to be smoothed out a bit. Cook until slightly browned. Serve with ginger butter.

Yield: 12 pancakes

Ginger Butter
½ cup soft butter
1½ tablespoons finely chopped candied ginger

Editors' Note: *The combination of sweet potatoes and pecans characterize this as a "deep South" variation of pancakes.*

"Total Southern elegance enhanced by a hospitable, knowledgeable staff."
-- Jim Kott, *America's Favorite Inns, B&Bs, and Small Hotels*

"An eclectic mix of styles makes this distinctive brick house one of Savannah's finest mansions and an outstanding inn in a city known for its historic guest houses." -- *Georgia Journal*, 1997

"In a city characterized by grand homes and beautiful inns, The Kehoe House distinguishes itself as a delightful combination of the two."
-- *Best Read Guide* Savannah, August 1999

"Elegant and expert at pampering guests, the Kehoe House is all you could hope for in a B&B and more."-- *Points North*, October 2000

17 Hundred 90

Captures the authentic flavor of Georgia's first and most romantic city

Address: 307 E. President Street
Savannah, GA 31401
(Historic District)
Telephone: (912) 236-7122
Web Site: www.17hundred90.com

Cuisine: American Regional
Executive Chef: Debbie Reid
Price Range: Lunch/$6.75-$9.25
Dinner/$16.50-$25.95

Veal Medallions with Lemon Caper Butter

8 veal medallions, cut ¾ inches
  thick from center loin
1-2 tablespoons of olive oil
Seasoned flour
¼ cup white wine (not a sweet wine)
½ lemon (or more, if preferred), juiced

1 small can artichoke
  hearts, drained
1-2 tablespoons of capers
Salt and pepper, to taste
1 stick unsalted butter,
  cut into small pieces

Cover veal with plastic wrap and pound, with a meat mallet, to less than ¼ inch thick. Preheat oven to 180°. Heat a sauté pan and add olive oil after pan is hot, but not smoking. Dredge veal lightly in flour, shaking off excess. Add medallions to sauté pan in batches, being careful not to crowd the pan. Cook until golden brown on both sides, about 1 to 2 minutes on each side. Add more olive oil, as needed. When done, place meat on an oven-proof platter and keep warm. After all medallions are cooked, deglaze pan with wine and lemon juice; cook until reduced. Add remaining ingredients. Whisk butter into sauce and continue whisking until butter is incorporated and sauce is creamy. Spoon sauce over veal medallions and serve.

Yield: 4 servings

Editors Notes: *Capers are found with the condiments in a super market. The lemon caper butter is the crowning glory of this wonderful veal dish.*

Restaurants
Savannah, Georgia
❧❧❧❧❧❧❧❧❧❧❧❧❧❧❧❧❧❧❧❧❧❧❧❧❧❧❧

Roasted Rack of Lamb

2 racks of lamb, Frenched	1 teaspoon olive oil
Salt and pepper, to taste	½ cup red wine

Preheat oven to 425°. Salt and pepper racks and set aside. Add oil to skillet and add lamb when oil is hot (almost smoking). Sear meat-side down about 2 minutes to brown. Turn over, when meat freely loosens, and sear same amount of time on other side. Attempt to brown all sides, including ends. When lamb is well-seared, take out and let cool. Pour off excess fat and deglaze pan for sauce by adding wine and scraping all browned bits off bottom of pan. Set aside.

Mustard Coating

1½ tablespoons Dijon mustard	2 teaspoons fresh rosemary
1½ tablespoons grain mustard	1 teaspoon Lawry's seasoning salt
2 cloves fresh garlic, chopped	¼ teaspoon freshly ground pepper

Combine all ingredients. Using a pastry brush, apply coating over entire surface of meat (except the bones).

Bread Crumbs

½ cup seasoned bread crumbs   ½ teaspoon garlic powder   ½ teaspoon dry mustard

Roll coated lamb into seasoned bread crumbs. Pan spray or coat with oil an oven-proof pan and put lamb in pan, rack side down. Place in preheated oven. While lamb is cooking, finish preparing sauce (below). Using a meat thermometer, cook lamb to desired temperature or 130° for rare (about 15 to 20 minutes). Take out of oven and let sit for 5 to 10 minutes. Internal temperature will continue to increase 5 to 10 degrees. Cut between the ribs and divide lamb into 4 servings.

Sauce

1½ cup beef stock   Kitchen Bouquet, optional

Add stock (lamb or veal) to skillet where deglazing has been done. Simmer liquid down to about ⅓ to thicken sauce, leaving approximately 1 cup of sauce. Season to taste with salt and pepper; add a little Kitchen Bouquet to darken, if desired. Serve over sliced lamb.

Yield: 4 servings

Editor's Note: *Add 1 teaspoon butter to sauce, melt, and stir in before serving. Delicious served with roasted rosemary-scented potatoes and baby peas sautéed with shallots.*

Georgia Trend magazine singled out 17 Hundred 90
as a favorite spot for "financiers, business people, and professionals."

17 Hundred 90 has been a gourmet tradition in Savannah
for over a century and has been acclaimed as
"the most elegant restaurant in Savannah" by *Gourmet Magazine*

45 Bistro

Reflective of Savannah's class and style

Address: The Marshall House
123 E. Broughton St.
(Historic District)
Telephone: (912) 234-3111
Web Site: www.marshallhouse.com/dining.shtml

Cuisine: Eclectic
Executive Chef: Ryan Behneman
Price Range: Dinner/$15-$28

Grilled Caesar Salad

Caesar Dressing

1½ teaspoons Worcestershire sauce
1 egg yolk
2 cloves fresh garlic, minced
1 tablespoon Dijon mustard
1½ ounces anchovy filet, optional

½ cup red wine vinegar
½ cup Parmesan cheese, shredded
2 cups canola or olive oil
Salt & freshly ground pepper, to taste
Juice from ½ lemon

Blend first 5 ingredients in food processor until paste is formed. Add next 2 ingredients and blend. Slowly and evenly add salad oil. Add remaining ingredients and blend. Cover and chill until ready to use.

Salad

Heart of romaine lettuce   ½ pound Asiago cheese   ½ cup seasoned croutons

Cut lettuce in half lengthwise, leaving bottom in tact so it holds together. Coat romaine halves with Caesar dressing in a bowl. Place coated romaine onto a hot grill a couple of minutes or until grill marks appear. Flip romaine and mark (with grill pattern) the other side. Arrange lettuce on a plate and top with shaved Asiago cheese (see note on page 129) and croutons.

Yield: 2 servings

Editors' Notes: *Shave cheese into strips using a vegetable peeler. Use your favorite recipe for croutons or buy them already prepared.*

Filet of Salmon Gratinéed with Asiago Cheese

Small can of hearts of palm
Small can artichoke hearts, quartered
Olive oil
Salt & pepper, to taste

3 pounds filet of salmon
1½ cups white wine
1½ cups Asiago cheese, grated
Paprika for garnishing

Preheat oven to 350°. Cut hearts of palm into ½-inch pieces and sauté with artichokes in olive oil; salt and pepper to taste. Keep warm. Place salmon in pan, cover with wine, and top with cheese. Cook for 9 to 11 minutes until fish is firm, basting occasionally. When ready, cheese should be melted and slightly brown. Place salmon on plate and top with artichokes and heart of palms. Garnish with paprika.

Yield 6 servings

Editors' Notes: *Asiago (ah-SYAH-goh) is an Italian cheese with a rich, nutty flavor—it is succulent melted on top of the salmon. This dish is also good served over ratatoille (ra-tuh-TOO-ee), as it is served at 45 Bistro. Trout may be substituted for salmon.*

Prince Edward Island Mussels with a Citrus Lemon Grass Coconut Milk

1 pound live mussels
Zest (grated peel) and juice of 1 lime
Zest (grated peel) and juice of 1 lemon
2 tablespoons lemon grass, chopped

2 tablespoons peeled, chopped ginger
3 ounces coconut milk
½ cup white wine

Wash shells of mussels and scrub down in cold water. Put aside. Combine all ingredients and pour into a sauté pan immediately after adding mussels to hot sauté pan. Cover pan with lid. Cook on high heat for 3 to 4 minutes until mussels open up. Throw away any mussels that do not open. Pour liquid from sauté pan over mussels to serve.

Yield 2 servings

Editors' Notes: *If mussels (or clams) do not open up, they are not alive and must be discarded. Lemon grass can usually be found fresh in produce department or chopped in frozen section of grocery store. Use only the brown root part of lemon grass, not the green part. Peel fresh ginger with a teaspoon; chop and freeze, in advance, to have ready at time of preparation. Coconut milk is found in canned goods area of grocery stores. Clams may be substituted for mussels, but they may need to be cooked longer. Lemon grass is an important herb in Thai and Vietnamese cooking. Use the white base (up to where leaves start) for flavoring this recipe and discard before serving. If unavailable, use a little extra lemon zest.*

"Everything is a winner at 45 Bistro."
--*Savannah Morning News* (April 5, 2002)

Belford's

Casual dining in City Market

Address: 315 W. St. Julian St.
Savannah, GA 31401
(City Market)
Telephone: (912) 233-2626
Web Site: www.savannahcitymarket.com/
belfords

E-mail: BelfordsSav@aol.com
Cuisine: American regional
Executive Chef: George Denmark
Price Range: Breakfast/$4.95-$12.95
Lunch/$6.95-$12.95
Dinner/$16.95-$24.95

Grouper Anglais

Vegetable cooking spray
1 cup panko bread crumbs
½ teaspoon dried thyme
½ teaspoon dried marjoram
1 pound grouper filets
Salt and pepper, to taste

1 tablespoon clarified butter
½ medium onion, diced
1 cup diced peppers
(green, red, and/or yellow)
1 cup Chardonnay or other white wine
½ cup cooked crabmeat

Preheat oven to 350°. Spray a baking sheet with vegetable cooking spray and set aside. In a shallow bowl or plate, mix the first 3 ingredients. Lightly season the filets with salt and pepper; dredge in bread crumb mixture, shaking off any excess. Place filets on baking sheet. Bake until cooked through, about 10 to 12 minutes. While filets bake, heat the clarified butter in a large non-stick pan over medium heat. Add onion and peppers and sauté until tender, about 7 minutes. Add wine and simmer for 2 to 3 minutes more, stirring occasionally. Stir in crabmeat and heat through. Serve filets topped with the wine and crabmeat sauce.

Yield: 2 servings

Editors' Notes: *Clarified butter, also referred to as drawn butter, is an unsalted butter that has been slowly melted and the milk solids skimmed out. Panko bread crumbs are larger, coarser crumbs often used in Japanese cooking and provide a delicious crunchy crust. They are available in the Oriental section of many grocery stores or in Asian markets. Grouper may be substituted with sea bass, tilapia, or catfish filets..*

Restaurants
Savannah, Georgia

Parmesan Tomato Stack

Vegetable cooking spray
½ cup shredded Parmesan cheese
¼ cup extra-virgin olive oil
¾ cup balsamic vinegar
1 cup mozzarella cheese, shredded

½ cup panko bread crumbs
1 tablespoon dried oregano
1 tablespoon dried basil
6 large, ripe tomatoes (unpeeled and sliced about ½-inch thick)

Preheat oven to 450°. Combine oil and vinegar; set aside. Combine cheeses, bread crumbs and herbs. Lightly coat a baking sheet with vegetable cooking spray. Arrange tomato slices on the baking sheet, leaving at least ½ inch between them. Generously sprinkle bread crumb mixture on each tomato slice. Place another slice of tomato on top of each and top with more bread crumb mixture. Bake 3 to 5 minutes or until bread crumb mixture is lightly browned. Remove from oven and drizzle each tomato stack with the oil and vinegar dressing. Serve immediately.

Yield: 6 servings

Belford's Bread Pudding

1 egg
2 cups milk
¼ cup white sugar
¼ cup packed brown sugar
1 stick butter, melted
1 teaspoon nutmeg

1 tablespoon vanilla
1 teaspoon cinnamon
3 cups cubed bread
1 cup golden raisins
½ cup pecans or walnuts, optional

Preheat oven to 350°. Lightly grease an 8 or 9-inch square baking dish and set aside. Lightly beat egg in a large bowl. Add next 7 ingredients and stir to combine. Add cubed bread, stirring to coat well. Allow bread to soak for at least 10 minutes, stirring once or twice, to ensure it absorbs liquid mixture. Stir in raisins and nuts (if using) and spread mixture into greased baking dish. Bake until firm (a knife inserted in middle should come out clean) about 40 to 45 minutes. Cool, slightly, before serving.

Yield: 6 servings

Editors' Note: *We like this dish topped with warm caramel sauce (buy in ice-cream section of grocery store), a dollop of whipped cream, and a sprinkling of extra nuts.*

"The Grouper Anglaise was stuffed with a tasty flavorful blue crabmeat ... Every bite was a sheer joy." --*Creative Loafing*, January 13, 2001

Winner of "Best Menu Item" at the inaugural Taste of Savannah (January 26, 2001) for the Crab Cakes.

The Boar's Head

Casual fine dining, in an old cotton warehouse, overlooking the Savannah River

Address: 1 North Lincoln Street
Savannah, GA 31401
(Waterfront)
Telephone: (912) 651-9660
Web Site: http://savannahmenu.com/
boarshead

Cuisine: New American Cuisine
with a Southern Flair
Executive Chef: Philip Branan
Price Range: Lunch/$8-$15
Dinner/$15-$25

Philip Branan's Black-Eyed Pea Soup

¾ pound dried black-eyed peas
¼ pound bacon, diced
1 cup white onion, chopped
1 cup celery, chopped
1 cup carrot, chopped
2 cloves garlic, minced
¾ cup tomatoes, diced, with juice
1 cup fresh collards, rinsed,
stems removed, diced

1½ quarts rich chicken stock
1 smoked ham hock
½ teaspoon kosher salt
¼ teaspoon dried oregano
⅛ teaspoon dried thyme
⅛ teaspoon ground white pepper
½ cup cooked ham, diced
1½ teaspoon chopped fresh cilantro
1 ounce sherry

Soak peas overnight in cold water. Melt down bacon's fat, over medium heat, in a large, heavy-bottom soup pot. Add next 3 ingredients and cover. Cook until onions are soft, about 10 minutes. Add garlic and cook about 10 seconds. Drain peas and add to the pot, along with tomato and collards. Cover with stock and add ham hock; season with next 4 ingredients. Bring to a boil. Reduce heat to low and simmer, covered, for about 1½ hours. Remove ham hock and dice any meat left on bone. Return ham hock to pot, along with diced ham and cilantro. Finish with sherry and adjust seasonings, if necessary.

Yield: 8 cups

Editors' Note: *Ideal to serve on New Year's Day with hot, buttered cornbread.*

❧❧❧❧❧❧❧❧❧❧❧❧❧❧❧❧❧❧❧❧❧❧❧

Boar's Head Grill and Tavern Savannah Trifle

Vanilla Custard Sauce

1 cup sugar	8 egg yolks
1 quart heavy cream	1 tablespoon vanilla
Dash of salt	1 tablespoon Grand Marnier

Combine first 3 ingredients in a heavy-bottom pot. Scald. Place yolks in a stainless steel bowl and whip until lemon-colored. Once cream is scalded, slowly pour half of cream into yolks, whipping slowly. Next, temper (gradually add) yolk mixture back into remaining cream-- slowly whipping, all the while. This tempering process prevents yolks from scrambling. Put mixture back over low heat; cook, stirring with a wooden spoon, until custard has thickened and sticks to back of spoon. Remove from heat and add last 2 ingredients. Cool completely before assembling.

Assembly

1 (20-ounce) sponge cake, torn into pieces	Whipped cream
1½ ounces of Grande Marnier	Sliced almonds, toasted

Ladle 1½ cups sauce into bottom of an 8-inch crystal bowl. Top with a layer of cake, sprinkle Grand Marnier over cake, and repeat process (sauce/Grand Marnier/cake) for two more layers. Top cake on third layer with Grand Marnier, custard, whipped cream, and toasted almonds. Fruit, such as sliced strawberries, may be added for a festive touch. Refrigerate until time to serve.

Yield: 8-10 servings

Editors' Notes: *Grand Marnier (GRAN mahr-NYAY) is a rich, cognac-based, orange-fla- vored liqueur. Trifles are a specialty dessert of the Lowcountry, and this one is superb.*

In *Romantic Days and Nights in Savannah (2001)*,
Georgia Byrd cites The Boar's Head as Savannah's
"Most Romantic Restaurant"

"Great black-eyed pea and ham soup--
everything is made from scratch, the old-fashioned way!"
--*Savannah Magazine*, June 1999

The first restaurant on Savannah's famous River Street

Bodi's Sophisticated Palate and Homemade Desserts

A delightful find on Savannah's Southside

Address: 238 Eisenhower Drive
Savannah, GA 31406
Telephone: (912) 355-6160
Web Site: www.eatinginsavannah.com/
bodis.html
Cuisine: All types

Proprietor: Richard Halperin
Price Range: Breakfast/$3.95-$7.95
Lunch/$5.95-$8.95
Note: Also sells specialty gourmet
food products and cooking aids.

Curried Chicken Salad with Mango and Cashews

3 pounds chicken breasts, poached
(discard skin and bones; cut meat
into bite-size pieces, about 4 cups)
2 tablespoons fresh lemon juice
2 mangoes, peeled, pitted, and
cut into ¾-inch pieces
1 cup chopped celery
4 scallions, including green part, minced

¼ cup plain yogurt
¼ cup mayonnaise
1½ teaspoons curry powder
½ teaspoon ground cumin
1 cup roasted cashew nuts, chopped
2 tablespoons chopped
fresh coriander, if desired
Salad greens

In a large bowl, toss together first 3 ingredients. Add next 2 ingredients. In a small bowl, whisk together next 4 ingredients. Add dressing to chicken mixture with salt and pepper to taste. Mix salad together well. Just before serving, stir in cashews and coriander. Serve the salad, at room temperature or chilled, arranged atop salad greens.

Yield: 6 servings

Editors' note: *Coriander leaves are also known as cilantro. Grapes and walnuts may be substituted for mangoes and cashews.*

Richard's Oatmeal Cookies

1½ cups sifted flour	2 eggs
1 teaspoon salt	1 teaspoon vanilla extract
1 teaspoon baking soda	3 cups rolled oats
1 cup butter	1 cup chopped pecans
1 cup packed brown sugar	1 cup raisins, optional
1 cup sugar	

Sift together the first 3 ingredients. Cream butter and sugars in a mixing bowl until light and fluffy. Beat in eggs. Add sifted dry ingredients and mix well; stir in vanilla. Blend in remaining ingredients. Drop by teaspoonfuls onto greased cookie sheets and bake at 350° for 10 to 15 minutes, or until lightly browned.

Yield: 3 dozen medium-sized cookies

Editors' note: *Make a double batch and keep the extra dough in the freezer for next time. This is a cookie that your family will want you to fix again.*

Two-Version Praline Cheesecake
Graham Cracker Crust

1 cup graham cracker crumbs	¼ cup butter, melted
¼ cup finely chopped pecans	

Combine all ingredients in a bowl and mix well. Press over the bottom of a 9-inch springform pan. Chill.

Filling

24 ounces cream cheese, softened	2 teaspoons vanilla extract
1¼ cups packed brown sugar	1 cup whipping cream
3 eggs	

Beat cream cheese in a mixing bowl until light and fluffy. Gradually beat in 1 cup of sugar. Beat in the eggs 1 at a time, mixing well after each addition. Stir in remaining ingredients and pour into prepared crust. Sprinkle top with remaining ¼ cup brown sugar. Bake at 450° for 10 minutes and then reduce temperature to 275°. Bake 1 hour. Cool on a wire rack. Remove side of the pan and place onto a serving plate.

Yield: 10-12 servings

Featured in the *Savannah Morning News*
May 30, 1999

Downtown Café at Main

Quiet, Romantic, Subtle

Address: 1 Broughton Street
Savannah, GA 31401
(Historic District)
Telephone: (912) 233-8666
Web Site: www.downtowncafeatmain.com

Cuisine: International/Continental
Executive Chef: Laxman Khatri
Price Range: Lunch/$5.95-$14.95
Dinner/$9.95-$22.95

Snapper Francese with Creamy Lemon Wine Sauce

4 snapper filets (6-8 ounces each)
½ teaspoon salt (or to taste)
¼ teaspoon freshly ground pepper
Lemon juice from 1 lemon (no seeds or pulp)

1 cup all-purpose flour
1 egg (for egg wash)
3 tablespoons vegetable oil for frying

Prepare Creamy Lemon Wine Sauce (p.137) and keep warm. Season filets with first 3 ingredients and marinate for 15 minutes. Dredge filets in flour (seasoned with salt and pepper, to taste) and dip into egg wash (egg + 2 tablespoons water). Have a pan (preheated over medium heat) ready with enough oil to coat bottom of pan (no more than ⅛–inch). Add the filets to pan without any overlapping or touching. Sauté on one side until golden, and then turn and sauté on other side; only turn filets once. Add more oil, as needed. Continue sautéing until done (should be moist and flaky). Serve immediately with Creamy Lemon Wine Sauce.

Yield: 4 servings

Restaurants
Savannah, Georgia

Beef Stroganoff

Olive oil (enough to coat pan)
1½ pounds beef tenderloin,
    cut in strips
Salt and pepper, to taste
2 medium onion, sliced
1½ cups sliced mushrooms
3 cloves garlic, chopped

1½ -2 cups brown stock
¾ cup red wine
1½ teaspoons roux
4 tablespoons gherkins,
    chopped for garnish (optional)
4 cups cooked rice or noodles, drained
    (add salt to water after it begins boiling)

Preheat a large skillet over medium heat for 3 to 4 minutes, then turn heat up to high and add oil. Season tenderloin strips with salt and pepper and add to skillet, arranged in a single layer. Sauté, without stirring, until well-browned but still pinkish inside. Transfer meat to a large plate and set aside. Repeat with remaining meat, adding more oil if needed. Add next 3 ingredients and sauté until onions are translucent and mushrooms browned. Remove to same dish as beef. Start cooking noodles or rice. Deglaze pan with wine, scraping all browned bits until dissolved. Add stock, return to simmer, and reduce by almost one-half. If a thicker sauce is desired, add roux by whisking in a little bit at a time. Return beef and sautéed vegetables, along with any drippings, to sauce just long enough to bring to serving temperature. Serve over cooked noodles or rice and garnish stroganoff with chopped gherkins.

Yield: 4 servings

Editors' Notes: *Ask your butcher to slice tenderloin into strips (¼-inch thick x ½-inch wide x 1½-inches long). For a richer variation, stir in ½-1 cup sour cream into sauce before returning beef to pan. When serving stroganoff over noodles, we like to toss the noodles with butter, parsley and dill. If desired, garnish the stroganoff with parsley instead of gherkins (GER-kihns), a variation of a cucumber.*

Creamy Lemon Wine Sauce

4 teaspoons lemon juice
⅓ cup white wine
2 tablespoons half-and-half

4 tablespoons butter, cut into ½-cubes
1½ teaspoons roux (see page 139)
    (or corn starch slurry), optional

Bring lemon juice and wine to a simmer in a small sauce pan. Whisk in half-and-half and slightly reduce mixture. Lower heat, then whisk in butter (in small amounts, 1 or 2 pieces at a time) until butter is incorporated and sauce is creamy and smooth. If desired, whisk in roux (ROO) or corn starch slurry to thicken further. Avoid overheating to keep sauce from separating. Keep warm, whisking occasionally until served with filets.

Editors' Notes: *Simmer ¼ cup chopped shallots with lemon juice and wine for extra flavor. "Cornstarch slurry," a thickening agent, is prepared by mixing equal parts of cornstarch and cold water.*

Highly recommended in *The Food Scoop.*

Johnny Harris Restaurant

Serving the "Best Barbeque" since 1924

Address: 1651 E. Victory Drive
        Savannah, GA 31404
Telephone: (912) 354-7810
Web Site: www.johnnyharris.com

Cuisine: American
Executive Chef: Joseph Marinaro
Price Range: Lunch/$4.95-$9.50
                  Dinner/$9.95-$23.85

Steak Au Poivre

½ cup black peppercorns
5 tablespoons olive oil
2 tablespoons, plus 1 teaspoon butter
4 (¼-inch thick) strip steaks,
    thinly cut

¼ cup minced shallots
¼ cup cognac (or brandy)
½ cup rich beef stock
4 tablespoons chopped tarragon
Salt and pepper, to taste

Crack peppercorns by crushing them against a cutting board with side of a heavy knife or bottom of a pan or grind them in a pepper mill. Press peppercorns into sides of steaks. Heat oil with 2 tablespoons of butter in a heavy skillet. Cook steaks, turning occasionally, until cooked to desired doneness. Remove steaks from pan and keep warm while preparing sauce. Add shallots to pan and sauté until translucent. For next step, be careful as cognac creates a large flame. Add cognac (or brandy) to skillet and light with a match. Shake pan above burner until flame dies out. Add beef stock and cook over high heat. Whisk in remaining butter and tarragon. Season to taste with salt and pepper. Serve sauce over steaks.

Yield: 4 servings

Editors' Notes: *N.Y. strips work well for Steak Au Poivre (oh PWAHV-r). Poivre is French for "pepper."*

❧❧❧❧❧❧❧❧❧❧❧❧❧❧❧❧❧❧❧❧❧❧❧❧❧

BBQ Shrimp Stir-Fry

2 pounds shrimp, peeled and cooked
1 cup broccoli florets
1 cup cauliflower florets
1 cup sliced carrots

1 cup cherry tomatoes
1 cup sliced mushrooms
1 cup Johnny Harris BBQ sauce

Combine all ingredients in a wok, pour barbecue sauce over top, and stir until vegetables are tender and cooked through.

Yield: 4-6 servings

Editors' Notes: *A wok is a round-bottomed cooking pan often used in Asian cooking, especially with stir-frying. Serve BBQ Shrimp with rice.*

Grilled Pork Steaks

6 ounces beer
2 tablespoons of margarine
3 bay leaves
Salt and white pepper, to taste

Ground garlic
4 pork steaks
1 cup Johnny Harris BBQ sauce

Pour beer into a sauce pan; add margarine and seasonings. Allow mixture to simmer. Trim away all but a small amount of fat from the edges of meat and score edges in several places (prevents meat from curling). Grill steaks for 15 to 20 minutes over medium-high heat, turning frequently. Brush on sauce after each turn and on both sides immediately before removing from grill.

Yield: 4 servings

Editors' Notes: *Try serving pork steaks with a baked Vidalia onion--cored, stuffed with butter and a beef bouillon cube; and bake at 350° (or microwave) until tender. Johnny Harris BBQ sauce may be ordered online (www.johnnyharris.com) or by calling 1-888-547-2823*

Johnny Harris BBQ sauce chosen "favorite sauce"
in nation-wide contest. -- *Bon Appetit* (1996)

"To enter the door at Johnny Harris Restaurant
is to step back to a time when eating out was a special treat."
--Richard Allen, *Savannah Morning News* (1997)

The Lady and Sons

Good home cooking in an atmosphere of true Southern hospitality

Address: 102 W. Congress St.
Savannah, GA 31401
(Historic District)
Telephone: (912) 233-2600
Web Site: www.ladyandsons.com
Cuisine: Southern

Proprietor: Paula H. Deen
Price Range: Lunch/$5.99-$14.99
Dinner/$14.99-$21.99
Cookbook: *The Lady & Sons*
Savannah Country Cookbook
(+ 2 more)

Bubba's Beer Biscuits

2 cups Bisquick
¼ cup sugar

½ can beer (6 ounces)
1 tablespoons butter, melted

Preheat oven to 400°. Mix ingredients well, adjusting the sugar according to how sweet a biscuit you prefer. Spoon into well-greased muffin tins. Bake for 15 to 20 minutes. Serve with Molasses Pecan Butter (page 35).

Yield: 10 medium-sized biscuits

Editors' Notes: *We prefer rolling dough out and cutting it into rounds with a biscuit cutter. For a delicious batch of cheese beer biscuits, omit the sugar and add 1 cup grated sharp Cheddar cheese plus 1½-2 teaspoons of garlic salt, depending on taste..*

Squash Casserole

2 cups cooked, mashed yellow squash
2 cups Ritz cracker crumbs
1 cup evaporated milk
1 cup shredded cheese,
such as Cheddar or Swiss
1 cup onion, chopped

2 eggs, lightly beaten
1 teaspoon salt
1 teaspoon pepper
Pinch of sugar
6 tablespoons butter

Place squash in a large bowl. Add next 4 ingredients and stir well. Stir in remaining ingredients and pour into a greased 1-quart casserole. Bake at 350° for 40 minutes.

Yield: 4 servings

Baked Spaghetti

Sauce

1 cup canned diced tomatoes	2 tablespoons chopped fresh parsley
1 cup tomato sauce	¾ teaspoon Italian seasoning
½ cup water	¾ teaspoon The Lady's seasoned salt
¼ cup diced onions	¾ teaspoon The Lady's House seasoning
¼ cup diced green pepper	¾ teaspoon sugar
1 clove garlic, chopped	1 small bay leaf

Combine all ingredients in a stockpot and bring to a boil. Reduce heat and simmer, covered, for 1 hour.

Beef and Pasta

¾ pound ground beef	½ cup Cheddar cheese, grated
1 pound uncooked angel hair pasta	½ cup Monterey Jack cheese, grated

Crumble ground beef in a saucepan and cook until no pink remains; drain off fat. Add the browned beef to stockpot and simmer for another 20 minutes. While sauce simmers, cook pasta according to package directions. Cover bottom of a 13 x 9 x 2-inch pan with sauce, a layer of pasta, and one-half of the cheese. Repeat layers and end with the sauce. Bake at 350° for 30 minutes. Top with remaining cheese and return to oven. Continue cooking until cheese is melted and bubbly. Cut into squares before serving.

Yield: 4-5 servings

Editors' Note: *Lawry's seasoned salt may be substituted for The Lady's seasoned salt. The Lady's house seasoning may be made by stirring together 1 cup salt, ¼ cup black pepper, and ¼ cup garlic powder. Keep seasoning in a shaker.*

Ranked the "#1 International Meal in America for 1999" by Jerry Shriver, *USA Today*.

Featured on cover of *Savannah Magazine* (Sept.-Oct. 1999)

Paula Deen has appeared as a guest on

QVC	*Ready, Set, Cook*
Good Morning, America	*The Food Network*

Since November 2002, Paula Deen has hosted "Paula's Home Cooking" on *The Food Network*. It is the only show on the network led by a "down-home" Southern cook.

Mrs. Wilkes' Boarding House

Old-time family style dining

Address: 107 W. Jones Street
Savannah, GA 31401
(Historic District)
Telephone: (912) 232-5997
Web Site: www.mrswilkes.com

Cuisine: Home-style, Southern cooking
Proprietors: Marcia & Ronnie Thompson
Price Range: Lunch/$12
Cookbook: *Mrs. Wilkes' Boardinghouse
Cook Book* (+ 1 more)

Country Fried Steak

1½ pounds cubed steak
Worcestershire sauce
Salt & pepper, to taste
Pinch of garlic powder
Flour for dredging

¼ cup vegetable oil
½ cup minced onion
2 cups hot water
3 tablespoons flour

Place steak in a casserole dish and generously sprinkle with Worcestershire sauce. Cover and marinate overnight. Remove from marinade and generously sprinkle with salt, pepper, and garlic powder. Dip steak in flour and shake. Heat oil and quickly fry steak until brown, but do not cook inside too much. This is done by cooking both sides on high heat, turning quickly, and then reducing heat to low to finish cooking. Boil onion in another pot with ¼ cup of water for about 5 minutes. When finished cooking steaks, remove from pan; leave about 3 table-spoons browned crumbs (not burned) and drippings from steak in skillet. Add onion and 3 tablespoons flour. Stir until slightly browned. Slowly pour in the remaining hot water as it thickens. Season with salt and pepper to taste. The gravy may be served over rice or steaks.

Yield: 3-4 servings

Editors' Note: *Always a favorite with men and good served with vegetables on page 143.*

❧❧❧❧❧❧❧❧❧❧❧❧❧❧❧❧❧❧❧❧❧❧❧❧❧❧

Fried Okra

1½ pounds fresh okra	Flour
Salt and pepper	Corn oil (or other cooking oil)

Cut okra crosswise into ¾-inch slices. Season with salt and pepper. Toss okra in flour and shake off excess. Heat about ½ inch of oil in a skillet. Fry okra over medium heat. Stir and turn until light brown and tender. Remove with a spatula and drain on paper towels.

Yield: 4 servings

Savannah Red Rice

2 medium onions, diced	1 cup tomato sauce or catsup
2 medium green peppers, diced	½ teaspoon Tabasco sauce
Bacon drippings	4 strips bacon, fried to a crisp and crumbled
2 cups cooked rice	Salt and pepper
6-8 tomatoes	2 tablespoons grated Parmesan cheese
(peeled, chopped and cooked)	

Preheat oven to 325°. Brown first 2 ingredients in drippings. In a large mixing bowl, combine onions and peppers with next 5 ingredients. Salt and pepper, to taste. Mix well. Pour into a greased casserole dish and sprinkle with cheese. Bake for 30 minutes or until rice is dry enough to separate.

Yield: 4-6 servings

Editors' Notes: *Fresh tomatoes may be substituted with 1 (16-ounce) can tomatoes. The addition of 1 pound of cooked shrimp, ground beef, sausage, or ham will transform this Lowcountry classic into a delicious one-dish meal. Red rice is also good topped with grated Cheddar cheese. Garnish with parsley.*

Winner of the 2000 James Beard

"At age ninety-four she (Mrs. Wilkes: 1907-2002) is the queen of all the surveys, the grande doyenne of Southern dining." -- John T. Edge, 2000

Featured in *The Atlanta Journal, The Belgian Weekly Gazette, Bon Appetit, Esquire, The Boston Globe, The New York Times, Pittsburg Post-Gazette, Redbook, Savannah Morning News, Sky, Southern Living, Time, Town and Country,* and profiled on David Brinkley's evening news program.

Soho South Cafe

Where food is an art

Address: 12 W. Liberty Street
            Savannah, GA 31401
Telephone: (912) 233-1633
Web Site: www.sohosouthcafe.com

Cuisine: American comfort and European flair
Proprietress/Chef: Bonnie Retsas
Price Range: Lunch/$6.25-$9.75
            Sunday brunch/$3.95-$10.95

Crab and Asparagus Quiche

1 (10 inch deep-dish) pie shell
3 whole eggs
2 egg yolks
1 cup heavy cream
1 cup sour cream
1½ cups Gruyère cheese
1 whole shallot, minced,
     then sautéed in 1 teaspoon
     butter until soft; cooled
¼ cup Boursin cheese
1 tablespoon minced dill

1 tablespoon minced tarragon
1 teaspoon salt
¼ teaspoon white pepper
⅛ teaspoon cayenne
¼ teaspoon nutmeg
1 bunch fresh asparagus, trimmed
     and blanched for 3 minutes in
     boiling, salted water; cooled and
     sliced crosswise
½ pound jumbo lump crabmeat,
     picked over

Line pie shell on bottom and up the sides of a a deep-dish pie pan. Bake in 350° oven about 10 minutes or until crust is pale golden brown. Whisk together first 16 ingredients. Mix in asparagus and crab. Bake at 325° for 60 to 75 minutes, or until filling is set and no longer jiggles.

Yield: Serves 6-8

Editors' Notes: *Boursin (boor-SAHN) is a smooth, white cheese with a buttery texture. This quiche is good served with sliced cantaloupe or other fresh fruit.*

Restaurants
Savannah, Georgia

Mixed Berry Shortcakes

Shortcakes

1½ cups all-purpose flour	1 whole egg
½ rounded tablespoon baking powder	1 egg yolk
¼ teaspoon salt	1 cup heavy cream
¼ cup sugar, rounded	½ teaspoon vanilla
4 tablespoons butter, cubed	1½ teaspoons orange zest (rind)

Stir dry ingredients together in a large bowl. Cut butter into dry ingredients. Whisk remaining ingredients together in a smaller bowl. Mix egg mixture into dry ingredients using a rubber spatula (hold some of liquid back in case you don't need it all). Dough should be moist. Turn dough out onto floured surface; pat or roll into 1-inch thick circle. Cut into 8-9 rounds and place on a parchment-lined baking pan. Place in freezer for 15 minutes. Brush tops lightly with additional cream and sprinkle tops with extra sugar. Bake in 400° oven for approximately 17 to 20 minutes (or until a sharp knife inserted in center comes out dry).

Berries

1½ quarts of mixed berries
(strawberries, blueberries, raspberries, and blackberries)
½ cup sugar
Juice of half an orange

Slice strawberries and mix with remaining berries. Add sugar and juice of an orange. Let macerate (soak) for at least one hour or until sugar dissolves and juices are released from berries.

Whipped Cream

1 pint heavy cream   ¼ cup powdered sugar   ½ teaspoon vanilla

Beat together in cold bowl, with a cold whisk, until cream holds its shape.

To serve, spoon berries onto shortcakes and top with cream.

Yield: 4-5 servings

Editors' Note: *In addition to being delicious, this dish makes an attractive presentation.*

"Dinner at Soho South is an artistic triumph"
--Richard Allen, *Savannah Morning News*

*Selected as "1 of Top 500 Restaurants" in US by
2001 Chef's Guide to American Restaurants*

Toucan Cafe

A festive atmosphere with a little Caribbean, a little Greek Isles, a lot of whimsy

Address: 531 Stephenson Avenue
Savannah, GA 31406
Telephone: (912) 352-2233
Web Site: www.toucancafe.com

Cuisine: Eclectic
Executive Chef: Jim Leclair
Price Range: Lunch/$6-$10
Dinner/$10-$20

Eggplant Torte

1 medium to large eggplant
1 tablespoon salt
½ cup flour
Pinch thyme, basil, salt, and pepper
2 eggs
Cooking oil

8 ounces spinach, wilted
¼ cup creamy feta
1 tomato, sliced
1-1½ cup tomato basil sauce
Sliced provolone cheese
1 cup roasted orzo pasta

Peel and slice eggplant. Season with salt and let stand for 10 minutes; pat dry. Add seasonings to flour. Dip eggplant into flour and then into egg. Cook in lightly oiled pan (hot, but not smoking) until eggplant is lightly browned on both sides. Top each slice with spinach, creamy feta, and a stack of 3 tomatoes. Top with tomato sauce and cheese. Cook in 400° oven until cheese melts and center is warm (10 to 15 minutes). Serve over roasted orzo pasta.

Creamy Feta

12 ounces fresh feta cheese, crumbled
4-6 ounces heavy cream

Black pepper, to taste

In food processor, blend Feta (FEHT-uh) with next 2 ingredients until smooth.

Roasted Orzo Pasta

Place dried orzo (found in pasta section of grocery store) in 400° oven 8 to 10 minutes until browned.

Yield: 4-6

❧❧❧❧❧❧❧❧❧❧❧❧❧❧❧❧❧❧❧❧❧❧❧❧❧❧

Tilapia With Smoked Corn & Crawfish Relish

Crawfish Relish

1 pound smoked crawfish, veined and peeled

2 cups whole kernel corn, smoked

3-4 ounces hearts of palm, coarsely chopped

½ red pepper, finely diced

2 tablespoons cracked pepper

¾ cup green onions, finely chopped

1½ tablespoons pesto

2 tablespoons red wine vinegar

1 tablespoon extra virgin olive oil

Salt & fresh cracked pepper, to taste

Mix all ingredients together and chill in non-aluminum bowl until ready to serve.

Editors' Notes: *Small to medium-sized shrimp (shelled and deveined) may be substituted for crawfish (CRAY-fish). The amount of meat needed for this recipe is approximately 1½ cups.; save shells for making stock. A dash of liquid smoke may be used for flavoring corn.*

Red Pepper Sauce

2 roasted red peppers (or 1 12-ounce jar, drained)

4 tablespoons onion, coarsely chopped

3 green peppercorns

2¼ teaspoons garlic

Sweat onions and garlic in a small amount of oil until onion is translucent and tender. Mix onions and garlic with peppers in a blender. After blending well, add following ingredients:

1½ teaspoons fresh basil

¾ teaspoon fresh oregano

¼ teaspoon thyme

¼ teaspoon turmeric, optional

¼ cup chicken stock

Salt and pepper, to taste

Heat sauce to boil in same saucepan used to sweat onion and garlic. Reduce to a slow simmer and slightly reduce. If using dried herbs, instead of fresh, reduce amount by one-third.

Tilapia and Orzo

Salt and pepper

4 tilapia filets (6-8 ounce per serving)

Olive oil

½ pound orzo pasta

Salt and pepper tilapia. Sauté in oil in pan pre-heated over medium heat (avoid over-crowding). Turn once after 3 to 5 minutes; continue sautéing until done, adding additional oil as needed. Cook orzo by package directions.

Assembly

To serve, ladle Red Pepper Sauce into plate. Place a portion of orzo pasta in center of plate and top with tilapia. Garnish tilapia with Crawfish Relish that is cool, but not icy cold.

Yield: 4-6 servings

Editors' Notes: *A tablespoon of cream, added to pepper sauce just before serving, smooths out the flavors nicely. If relish and pasta are left over, mix together for a tasty luncheon salad.*

Featured in *Savannah Magazine*, July-August 1999.

Yanni's Greek Cuisine

A touch of the Greek Isles on Savannah's South Side

Address: 11211 Abercorn Street
Savannah, GA 31419
Telephone: (912) 925-6814
Web Site: http://savannahmenu.com/ yannis

Cuisine: Greek
Proprietor: Yanni Andronikos
Price Range: Lunch/$5~$10
Dinner/$12.95~$23.95

Mousaka

Béchamel Sauce

3½ tablespoons all-purpose flour
1 stick butter (4 ounces)

2 cups whole milk
Salt & white pepper, to taste

Combine ingredients in a sauce pan, whisking vigorously over high heat for 5 minutes or until sauce thickens. Place plastic wrap directly on surface of sauce, and set aside.

Vegetable and Meat Base

2 potatoes, sliced lengthwise, ¼-thick
2 medium eggplants, peeled and sliced
    sliced lengthwise, ¼ to ½-inch thick
Salt and pepper, to taste
Olive oil (enough for frying)
1 small onion, chopped

1 pound ground beef (or lamb)
¼ teaspoon ground cloves
1 small cinnamon stick
4 tablespoons tomato paste
½ cup whole, peeled, and chopped
    tomatoes (fresh or canned)

Sprinkle potato and eggplant slices with salt and pepper; sauté in olive oil until lightly brown and tender, adding additional oil, as needed. Remove slices from pan and drain on paper towels. Using same pan, sauté onion in a little oil until just tender. Add meat and next 2 ingredients; add more oil, as needed. After meat is browned, add tomato paste and then the tomatoes. Cook over low heat for 30 minutes or until all liquid is reduced. Remove cinnamon. In a 10-inch casserole dish, layer ingredients in following order: potatoes, eggplant, meat, sauce (layer should be approximately one-half inch thick). Bake in oven at 350° to 375° for 30 minutes or until sauce browns. Remove and let stand for 15 to 20 minutes before serving.

Yield: 4 servings

Editors' Notes: *Use smaller eggplants (about 1 pound each) as they are less bitter than larger ones tend to be. To add a flavor variation to the mousaka (MOO-sah-kah), add 1 teaspoon of chopped garlic while sautéing the onions and a pinch of fresh ground nutmeg to meat while browning.*

❦❦❦❦❦❦❦❦❦❦❦❦❦❦❦❦❦❦❦❦❦❦❦❦

Youlbst
(Leg of Lamb)

Boneless leg of lamb, 4-6 pounds	3 tablespoons oregano
10 cloves of garlic, peeled	1 tablespoon fresh black pepper
1 cup extra virgin olive oil	1 tablespoon salt

Preheat oven at 325°. Stuff lamb with garlic cloves. Baste outside of lamb with remaining ingredients. Cook for 2 hours. Use drippings to make a light glaze for lamb.

Yield: 18 servings

Editors' Note: *Use a meat thermometer to accurately determine level of doneness. Remove lamb from oven when temperature level is 5 to 10 degrees before desired temperature is reached. Let meat sit, tented with foil, for 15 to 20 minutes before serving. This allows time for the temperature to rise and for the meat juices to set. A good choice when serving a large crowd.*

Grilled Octapodi

1 cup extra virgin olive oil	4 tablespoons oregano
4 tablespoons salt	Juice from 2 lemons
Fresh octopus, 2-3 pounds	

Oil and salt fresh octopus; hang to dry for 24 hours. Remove legs and char-grill them for 20 minutes. Baste with extra virgin olive oil, oregano and lemons.

Yield: 4 servings

Editors' Note: *Octapodi (oc-tah-POH-dee), a popular Greek dish, is often served as an appetizer at Greek restaurants.*

Voted "Savannah's Best Southside Restaurant"
by *Creative Loafing's* Readers' Poll

17 Street Inn

A unique B&B at the beach

Address: 12 17th Street
Tybee Island, GA 31328
Reservations: 1-888-999-0607
Telephone: (912) 786-0607
E-mail: hmr1@aol.com

Web Site: www.tybeeinn.com
Category: B&B
Proprietors: Helen Miltiades
Jim Morris
Rates: $90-$165 (seasonal)

Banana Nut Bread

1½ cups of mashed bananas (3 large)
¾ cup of vegetable oil
2 eggs
2 cups all-purpose flour

½ cup chopped pecans, optional
1 teaspoon baking powder
½ teaspoon salt
¾ cup sugar

Pre-heat oven to 325°. Mix first 3 ingredients in a large bowl with a wooden spoon. Stir in remaining ingredients. Pour into a greased loaf pan (9 x 5 x 3 or 8½ x 4½ x 2½). Bake until a wooden pick, inserted in center of bread, comes out clean—approximately 60 to 70 minutes. Cool 10 minutes before removing from pan. Let bread cool completely before slicing.

Yield: 1 loaf

Editors' Note: *This bread freezes nicely.*

Bed & Breakfasts and Historic Inns
Tybee Island, Georgia

Canadian Bacon Quiche

4 slices Canadian bacon	1 tablespoon parsley flakes
½ cup chopped onion	2 eggs
2 tablespoons all-purpose flour	1 (12-ounce) can evaporated milk
1 cup Cheddar cheese, grated	1 frozen pie shell, thawed

Pan fry bacon and chop into small pieces. Mix bacon with next 4 ingredients in a bowl. Mix eggs and milk in another bowl. Place dry mixture into uncooked pie shell and pour liquid mixture on top. Bake quiche (KEESH) at 350° for 30 to 45 minutes or until firm.

Yield: 6-8 servings

Editors' Notes: *Regular bacon may be substituted for Canadian bacon. The addition of chopped spinach is also good.*

Cheesy Breakfast Casserole

1 (12-ounce) can Pillsbury crescent rolls	2 cups sharp Cheddar cheese
1 pound sausage, mild or medium hot	6 eggs
2 cups Monterey Jack cheese	

Spray a 9 x 13-inch pan with baking spray and line pan with crescent rolls. Bake at 375 ° for 7 minutes. Fry or broil sausage. After draining, arrange in pan over baked crescent rolls. Place one cup Monterey jack cheese and 1 cup of Cheddar cheese over sausage. Beat eggs and pour over sausage (should be enough to fill in around sausage and cheese). Top with remaining cheese and bake 35 to 40 minutes.

Yield: 8-10 servings

Highly recommended by *The INNside Scoop* B&B newsletter.
--February 2003

Georges of Tybee

Where excellence prevails in food, service, and atmosphere

Address: 105 E. Highway 80 (1 mile, on left, past Lazaretto Creek Bridge)
Tybee Island, GA 31328
Telephone: (912) 786-9730

Web Site: www.georgesoftybee.com
Cuisine: New World Continental
Executive Chef: Robert Wood
Price Range: Dinner/$16-$24

Three Onion Bisque

3 medium shallots
1 large Vidalia (or sweet) onion
1 large Spanish onion
1 sprig rosemary
3 sprigs thyme
1 sprig sage
1 bay leaf

Olive or canola oil
3 tablespoons chopped garlic
⅓ cup Arborio rice, uncooked
¾ cup Madeira wine
3 cups chicken stock
2 cups heavy cream
Salt and white pepper to taste

Peel onions; cut off ends, cut in half crosswise, and rub lightly with oil. Salt and pepper onions; roast at 400° for about 30 minutes or until golden brown. Set aside. Prepare a bouquet garni by wrapping herbs and bay leaf in cheese cloth and tying it with a butcher's string. Preheat a large pot over medium heat. Add enough oil to cover bottom of pot; add roasted onions and garlic. Sauté for 3 minutes, stirring a couple of times. Add rice and the bouquet garni and continue sautéeing for 2 more minutes. Deglaze pan by adding the Madeira and stirring along bottom of pot. Reduce mixture by one-half, then add chicken stock. Simmer for 30 minutes. Add cream and simmer for another 15 to 20 minutes. Remove bouquet garni and squeeze liquid back into the soup. Purée soup in a blender in 4 or 5 batches, then place in a clean pot. Return bisque (bihsk) to stove over low heat, seasoning with salt and white pepper. If you prefer a thicker soup, reduce on low heat until desired consistency.

Yield: 4-6 servings

Editors' Notes: *Arborio (ar-BOH-ree-oh) rice is an Italian grain shorter and fatter than other short-grain rice (do not substitute regular rice for it) and often used for risotto. This soup is definitely worth the effort!*

❧❧❧❧❧❧❧❧❧❧❧❧❧❧❧❧❧❧❧❧❧❧

Skillet Seared Yellowfin Tuna
Rice Cakes

3 jalapeños, seeded and minced
½ cup of cilantro, chopped
2 eggs
2 teaspoons salt

½ cup flour
1 teaspoon baking powder
3 cups cooked Jasmine rice

Combine first 4 ingredients in a bowl. Add next 2 ingredients to make a thick paste, then fold in rice with a spatula. Form batter into one-half inch thick cakes and set aside.Combine first 4 ingredients in a bowl.

Orange Sauce

3 cups orange juice (without pulp)
2 tablespoons shallots, thinly sliced
1 teaspoon hot chili paste
½ cup heavy whipping cream

1 teaspoon wasabi paste
   (more or less, to taste)
½ cup mayonnaise
1 tablespoon water

Place first 2 ingredients in a stainless steel pan or pot and reduce to 1 cup. Over medium heat, add next 2 ingredients. Reduce to 1 cup; set aside and keep warm. In another bowl, combine last 3 ingredients and set aside for drizzling over tuna and rice cakes.

Sesame Seed Wilted Spinach and Yellowfin Tuna

Salt and pepper, to taste
6 (6-ounce) portions yellowfin tuna,
   cut into steaks
2 tablespoons olive oil

1 tablespoons butter
1 tablespoon sesame seeds
½ pound fresh spinach
¼ cup white wine

Preheat oven to 350°. In a medium hot pan, sear rice cakes until crispy on both sides. Finish cooking them in oven for about 10 minutes. Meanwhile, heat a cast iron or non-stick pan on high. Salt and pepper both sides of tuna steaks and sear them in olive oil, until desired doneness (rare to medium-rare is best). In another hot pan, toast sesame seeds in butter. Add spinach and wine; cook until wilted. Season with salt and pepper. Ladle about 1½ ounces of orange sauce onto each person's plate. Place spinach on top of sauce in middle. Set a rice cake on top of spinach. Cut tuna in half; place each half of tuna on each side of rice cake.

Yield: 6 servings

"The warmly lit interior, with its appealing bar,
is perfect for a romantic evening." --*Fodor's Travel Guide* (2001)

Featured in *Southern Living* magazine (April 2000)

Recipient of the prestigious "Silver Spoon Award" by *Georgia Trends* (2002)

"As you drive beneath the canopies created by moss-draped oak trees lining the roads of St. Simons Island, you feel stress flee your body. The pressures of the city and the crush of the working world simply can't survive in this sort of environment."
--Chuck Mavis, Lodging.com / Travelbase

◦৩◦৩◦৩◦৩◦৩◦৩◦৩◦৩◦৩◦৩◦৩◦৩◦৩◦

"The landscape of St. Simons, the most complete resort destination in the Golden Isles, consists of moss-draped oaks shading quiet lanes and creek-fed marshes where birds and other wildlife thrive."

--TownNews.com/Travel Guide, 2000

◦৩◦৩◦৩◦৩◦৩◦৩◦৩◦৩◦৩◦৩◦৩◦৩◦৩◦

"Through tunnels of ancient oaks, you can bike and drive the length of St. Simons, finding treasures at every turn. It's very much a vacation haven for families."

--Frommer's The Carolinas and Georgia, 6th Edition

◦৩◦৩◦৩◦৩◦৩◦৩◦৩◦৩◦৩◦৩◦৩◦৩◦৩◦

Using Spanish moss, one of St. Simon's most noted features, as a metaphor for its native region, James J. Kilpatrick pens: "An indigenous, indestructible part of the southern character; it blurs, conceals, softens and wraps the hard limbs of hard times in a fringe shawl."

Web Site for St. SImon's Island, GA
www.bgicvb.com

St. Simon's Island

"Serenity by the Sea"

Original artwork by Amy Moreno

*A landmark on St. Simon's Island, the lighthouse replaces
the island's first lighthouse, destroyed by retreating Confederate troops in 1862.*

Beach Bed & Breakfast

Overlooking the Atlantic Ocean, Beach Bed & Breakfast
offers stellar accommodations accented with style and comfort.

Address: 907 Beachview Drive
St. Simon's Island, GA 31522
Telephone: (912) 634-2800
E-mail: reserve@
beachbedandbreakfast.com

Website: www.beachbedandbreakfast.com
Category: B&B
Owner/Innkeeper: Joe McDonough
Rates: $220-$495 (seasonal)

Beach Bed & Breakfast Casserole

¾ cup seasoned Italian bread crumbs
1 pound sausage
½ cup mushrooms, sliced
4 eggs
1 cup whole milk

½ teaspoon mayonnaise
½ Vidalia onion, grated
½ teaspoon mustard
Salt and pepper to taste

Cover bottom of a greased Pyrex dish with bread crumbs. Sauté sausage; crumble and drain. Layer sausage and mushrooms over bread crumbs. Beat eggs and blend in next 3 ingredients. Stir in remaining ingredients and refrigerate overnight. Before baking, top with cheese. Bake in a 350° oven for at 35 to 45 minutes.

Yield: 6-8 servings

Editors' Note: *If Italian bread crumbs are unavailable, use regular breadcrumbs seasoned with Italian seasoning.*

Bed & Breakfasts
St. Simon's Island, Georgia

Strawberry Tea Scones with Cream

3 cups of self-rising flour
½ cup sugar
1 stick butter, cut into pieces

¾ cup buttermilk
1 cup fresh strawberries, chopped

Mix flour and sugar; cut butter into mixture with a pastry blender or fork. Make a well in center of flour. Add strawberries to buttermilk (until milk rises to 1 cup), then stir into flour mixture. Save any extra strawberries for topping. Knead flour mixture on a floured surface. Once kneaded, roll dough out to about a ⅜-inch thickness and turn to flour both sides. Use a small cookie or biscuit cutter to cut out biscuit-sized scones. Bake at 400° for 10 minutes. Cool on a rack.

Glazing

1 cup 10-X powdered sugar   ⅛ cup milk

Add powdered sugar to milk and mix until pasty. With a pastry brush, "paint" on glazing while scones are still warm

Heavy Whipping Cream

1 pint heavy whipping cream   ¼ cup sugar   1 teaspoon vanilla

Whip cream until stiff, adding sugar and vanilla. Serve with scones.

Yield: 2 dozen medium-sized scones

Editors' Note: *These incomparable tea scones (better than any we recall ever having in England or Scotland) are one of the afternoon delights served at "Lucille's Tea by the Sea" (located on main floor of Beach Bed and Breakfast) each Wednesday and Friday afternoon. Reservations may be made by calling 912-634-2800.*

Featured in *The Georgia Trend* magazine (October 2002)

Featured in *Private Pilot* (July 2003)

Featured on cover of *The INNside Scoop* B&B newsletter (July 2003)

"Gloria has a contagiously beautiful smile, and her concern with comfort is a tribute to all the staff at the Beach Bed & Breakfast."
--Georgia's *Good Life* magazine (April 2003)

JMac's

Casual dining at its finest on St. Simon's Island

Address: 407 Mallory Street
St. Simon's Island, GA 31522
Telephone: (912) 634-0403
Web Site: www.jmacsislandrestaurant.com

Cuisine: American accented
by "flavors of the world"
Chef: Frank Giannotti
Price Range: Dinner/$9-$28

Garlic and Maple Roasted Pork Chops

2 cloves garlic
1 small bunch of parsley
1 small sprig of fresh rosemary
⅓ cup of maple syrup

4 tablespoons vegetable oil
4 (12-ounce) double-cut pork chops
Salt and pepper, to taste

Chop first 3 ingredients, one-half of syrup, and 2 tablespoons of oil in food processor until a smooth paste forms. Preheat oven to 375°. Season pork chops with a pinch of salt and freshly cracked pepper. Brush mixture on both sides of chops. Heat remaining oil in skillet over medium heat. When oil is hot, sauté both sides of chops; place in oven. Brush chops with remaining maple syrup every 5 to 7 minutes until done. After 20 to 25 minutes, remove from oven and place on a serving plate covered with foil for 10 minutes before serving.

Yield: Serves 4

Editors' Notes: *A butcher can custom-cut chops for you upon request. Basically, double-cut pork chops are just extra-thick pork chops. Serve chops with Black-eyed Pea and Butternut Squash Hash (page 159) or your favorite side dish.*

Restaurants
St. Simon's Island, Georgia

Black-eyed Pea and Butternut Squash Hash

1 large butternut squash	1 small onion (diced)
Salt and pepper to taste	2 cups fresh or frozen black-eyed peas
2 tablespoons vegetable oil	(boiled until tender)
2 tablespoons butter	1 cup cooked greens (your favorite)

After cleaning, peeling, and dicing squash, boil for 5 to 7 minutes in salted water until tender. Strain and cool. Place oil and butter in skillet or sauté pan. Add onions and cook over medium high heat until translucent. Add butternut squash and cook approximately 5 minutes, stirring often. Add peas and chopped greens and cook about 5 more minutes until heated throughout and tender. Season with salt and pepper to taste. Place in serving bowl or casserole dish. Keep warm until main course is ready.

Yields: 4 servings

Editors' Notes: *See page 100 for an easy way to peel and prepare butternut squash. For extra flavor, cook greens and peas together with a ham hock or Goya's ham seasoning. Be sure to squeeze excess water from the greens; this will prevent them from being runny or soupy. Other vegetables may also be added, as desired. Corn and boiled (or roasted) peanuts are excellent additions.*

Best Ever Choco-Chip Macaroons

2 cups sugar	4 cups shredded coconut
¼ cup water	1 cup chocolate chips
6 egg whites	

Cook sugar and water to 245° (use a candy thermometer for accuracy). Whip egg whites to stiff peaks, then slowly pour hot sugar into egg whites; whip ten minutes until cool. Fold in coconut and chocolate chips. Using a tablespoon, drop mixture onto greased cookie sheet. Cook at 375° for 8 to 10 minutes until a light golden brown.

Yields: 2 dozen

Editors' Note: *This is a light and delicious sweet which we often use as a sample from Low-country Delights at book signings.*

> "For dinner, make reservations at the charming JMac's. After dinner, stroll down to the pier for a view of the St. Simons Lighthouse."
> --*Southern Living*, September 2000

159

Other Recipes

Recipes from Laurel Hill Plantation Bed & Breakfast

McClellanville, SC

Apple Egg Casserole

4 eggs, beaten
1½ cups milk
1 tablespoon sugar
1½ cups biscuit mix
1 (21-ounce) can apple pie filling
½ teaspoon cinnamon

⅛ teaspoon nutmeg
¼ teaspoon allspice
2 cups sharp Cheddar cheese, shredded
½ stick butter, melted
1 pound ground sausage,
   cooked and drained (optional)

Beat eggs and add next 3 ingredients, blending until smooth. Mix pie filling with spices and spread in a 13 x 9 x 2-inch baking dish. Sprinkle cheese over apple mixture and cover with batter. Add crumbled sausage, if desired. Pour melted butter over casserole and bake at 350° 50 to 60 minutes or until golden brown. Serve warm.

Yield: 8-10 servings

Editors' Note: *We like this casserole, one of our breakfast favorites, prepared without the sausage and served with Canadian bacon.*

Bacon Quiche Biscuit Cups

8 ounces cream cheese, softened
2 tablespoons milk
2 eggs
½ cup shredded Swiss cheese

2 tablespoons chopped green onions
1 (10-ounce) can refrigerated flaky biscuits
5 slices bacon, crisply cooked and
   finely crumbled

Preheat oven to 375°. Grease 10 muffin cups. In a small bowl, beat first 3 ingredients on low speed until smooth. Stir in next 2 ingredients and set aside. Separate dough into 10 biscuits and place 1 biscuit into each greased muffin cup. Firmly press dough into bottom of muffin cups and up sides, forming a ¼-inch rim. Place half of bacon in bottom of dough- lined muffin cups and spoon about 2 tablespoons of cheese mixture over bacon. Bake 20 to 25 minutes or until filling is set and edges of biscuits are golden brown. Sprinkle each cup with remaining bacon and press lightly into filling. Remove from pan.

Yield: 10 servings

Editors' Notes: *Use regular-sized biscuits, not oversized ones. Pre-cooked bacon pieces provide an easy substitute for the bacon and works well in this recipe.*

Baked Tomato Halves

4 large tomatoes
8 tablespoons butter or margarine,
   divided in half
½ cup finely chopped onion
2 teaspoons prepared mustard

1 teaspoon Worcestershire sauce
4 slices white bread,
   torn into coarse crumbs
4 teaspoons chopped parsley

Preheat oven to 350°. Wash tomatoes and remove stems; cut in half crosswise. Place tomatoes, cut side up, in shallow baking pan. In 4 tablespoons of hot butter in skillet, sauté onion until tender. Stir in mustard and Worcestershire. Spread onion mixture on tomatoes. Melt remaining butter in skillet; add bread crumbs and parsley. Sprinkle crumb mixture over tomatoes. Bake, uncovered, 20 minutes or until heated through and crumbs are golden brown.

Yield: 4 servings

Editors' Notes: *These tomatoes are especially good topped with Panko bread crumbs.*

Holiday Brunch Bake

½ pound bulk breakfast sausage
2 ounces chopped pimento, drained
½ (10-ounce) box frozen chopped spinach,
   defrosted and drained
½ cup all-purpose flour
⅛ cup Parmesan cheese
1½ teaspoons instant minced onion

¾ teaspoons Italian seasoning
¼ teaspoon seasoning salt
4 eggs
1 cup milk
½ cup shredded Cheddar
   or provolone cheese

Preheat oven to 425°. Cook sausage and drain. Sprinkle cooked sausage on bottom of greased 9 x 13-inch baking pan. Top with ½ jar pimento and spinach. In small bowl, combine next 6 ingredients. In large bowl, beat eggs and milk. Add flour mixture to egg mixture and beat well. Pour beaten mixture over spinach. Bake for 20 to 25 minutes or until set. Top with remaining pimento and Cheddar or provolone (proh-voh-LOH-nee) cheese. Bake 2 to 3 more minutes or until cheese melts. Cut into squares.

Yield: 5 servings

To order a copy of Jackie Morrison's cookbook, featuring her private collection of Laurel Hill Plantation recipes, send a check or money order for $8.50 (tax and postage included) and the address where the cookbook should be mailed to:

Jackie Morrison
Laurel Hill Plantation
P. O. Box 190
McClellanville, SC 29458

or order online at: www.thefoodscoop.com/LHPcoookbook.html

NOTE: *Jackie and Lee Morrison hosted a never-to-be-forgotten bed and breakfast inn (see page 8) for 14 years where memorable breakfasts were consistently served. Jackie, who served as president of the South Carolina Bed and Breakfast Association before retiring from innkeeping in 2002, compiled this cookbook at the insistence of her well-fed guests.*

Original artwork by Amy Moreno

Lowcountry Oyster Roast

One of the Lowcountry's most popular forms of entertainment, an oyster roast provides an opportunity for savoring roasted oysters, scenic views of sea and marsh, Spanish moss dangling from ancient Live Oaks, and a sense-of-place richly woven with tradition.

Plantation-style Roasted Oysters

1 bushel of fresh oysters

Pick up oysters the day you plan to serve them. Keep oysters cool, but do not store on ice. If oysters have not already been cleaned when purchased, wash them down with garden hose to remove as much mud as possible. Do not wash too much, or the (desired) salty flavor may be washed away.

Yield: 1 bushel of oysters serves 4-5 people

Editors' Notes: *Oysters are in season during the "r" months of September through April. Some guests will consider the oysters an appetizer, and others will eat them as the main course. Allow for this when planning your menu. Also, be sure to have plenty of food available for guests who are not oyster-eaters. The attire for an oyster roast is casual.*

Food Ideas for Main Course

Okra soup (page 96)	Red Rice (page 143)	Beer Biscuits (page 140)
Smoked ham, sliced	Potato Salad (page 163)	Lemon Squares (page 39)
Barbecue beef and/or chicken	Cole Slaw (page 163)	Praline cookies (page 163)

Condiments for Oysters
Melted butter
Lemon wedges
Ritz or saltine crackers
Cocktail sauce and/or catsup
(serve in oyster shells)

Drinks
Iced-tea
Soft drinks
Beer
Wine

Et Cetera
Oyster knives
Roll of paper towel or napkins
Containers for disposing oyster shells
Gloves--1 size fits all
(for holding oysters while opening them)

Cole Slaw

4 cups cabbage, shredded	⅓ cup sugar
½ cup mayonnaise, more or less as needed	1 cup pickle relish, drained
	1 medium carrot, grated

Mix all ingredients together until well-blended. Refrigerate before serving.

Yield: 4-6 servings

Home-style Potato Salad

1½ cups cubed, cooked potatoes	¾ teaspoon salt
¼ cup diced celery	⅛ teaspoon pepper
½ cup chopped pickles	⅛ teaspoon mustard
¼ cup chopped pimento	⅛ tablespoon vinegar or lemon juice
1 tablespoon minced onion, optional	¼ cup bell pepper, chopped
2 hard boiled eggs (chopped), optional	⅛ cup mayonnaise

Place all ingredients into a mixing bowl, except mayonnaise. Stir mayonnaise in lightly with a wooden spoon, mixing well. Add more pepper, if desired, and chill. Garnish with paprika.

Yields: 6 servings

Praline cookies

½ cup soft butter or margarine	1½ cups all-purpose flour
2 cups dark brown sugar	1 teaspoon vanilla extract
1 egg, beaten	1-1½ cups pecans, coarsely chopped

Mix together first 3 ingredients until creamy; stir in rest of ingredients. Refrigerate mixture until easy to handle. Heat oven to 375°. Shape dough into one-inch balls and place three inches apart on a greased cookie sheet. Using bottom of a tumbler, covered with damp cheese cloth, flatten balls until ⅛–inch thick. Bake twelve minutes or until done.

Yields: 3 dozen cookies

Editors' Note: *The recipes on this page were contributed by Mrs. Wilkes' Boarding House (see page 143) and ones the restaurant is often asked to prepare for Lowcountry oyster roasts held in the Savannah area. An order form for Mrs. Wilkes cookbook, "Mrs. Wilkes' Famous Recipes," is available at: www.mrswilkes.com/cookbook.htm.*

Very primitive, very easy, so very wonderful...

"I use empty oyster shells to hold cocktail sauce, and I always make a big pot of chili (for non-oyster eaters) which we keep warm on the oyster roast chimney. There is an old wash tub filled with Cokes, beer, and a bottle of wine sitting out. Lee dumps the oysters onto the sheet metal, over the hot fire, and covers them with a crocker sack that has been soaking in a bucket of water. The oysters steam to the desired doneness. Some people like them really cooked, but most people just want them warmed through. When the oysters are done, Lee shovels them onto our big picnic table, and everyone digs in."

--Jackie Morrison, Laurel Hill Plantation
Photo Credit: Lee Morrison

Maxine Pinson's
Potpourri of Ice-cream Recipes

Basic Vanilla Ice-Cream

2 (14-ounce) cans sweetened condensed milk
1 quart half-and-half

1 tablespoon, plus 1 teaspoon,
vanilla extract

Combine all ingredients, mixing well. Pour ice-cream mixture into freezer can of a 1 gallon hand-turned or electric freezer. Freeze according to manufacturer's instructions.

Yield: 2½ quarts

Variations

Black Forest Ice-Cream: Stir 1 (5.5-ounce) can chocolate syrup and 1(16 ½-ounce) can pitted Bing Cherries, drained and halved, into ice-cream mixture just before freezing.

Black Walnut Ice-Cream: Substitute 1½ teaspoons black walnut extract for vanilla. Add 2 cups of coarsely chopped black walnuts to ice-cream mixture before or during freezing.

Butter Pecan Ice-Cream: Add 1 tablespoon butter flavoring and 2 cups coarsely chopped toasted pecans to ice-cream mixture just before freezing.

Cherry Pecan Ice-Cream: Substitute 1 teaspoon almond extract for vanilla, and add ⅓ cup maraschino cherry juice to ice-cream mixture; freeze ice-cream as directed. Stir ¾ cup quartered maraschino cherries and ¾ cup chopped pecans into ice-cream after freezing.

Chocolate Malt Ice-Cream: Stir 2 cups chocolate malt balls, chopped coarsely in blender, into ice-cream mixture just before freezing.

Cinnamon Ice-Cream: Stir in 2 tablespoons ground cinnamon (more or less, according to personal taste) into ice-cream mixture just before freezing. When served, garnish with a cinnamon stick.

Coffee Ice-Cream: Combine ¾ cup hot water and 1 tablespoon instant coffee granules, stirring until granules dissolve. Let cool slightly. Stir coffee mixture into ice-cream mixture just before freezing.

Lemonade Ice-Cream: Add 1 (6-ounce) can frozen lemonade concentrate (yellow or pink), thawed and undiluted, to ice-cream mixture before freezing.

Maple Walnut Ice-Cream: Stir 1½ cups real maple syrup into ice-cream mixture before freezing. Pour in ¾ cups chopped walnuts during freezing process or stir in after freezing, while ice-cream is still soft.

Mint Chocolate Chip Ice-Cream: Stir ½ cup green crème de menthe and 1(6-ounce) package semi-sweet chocolate mini-morsels into ice-cream mixture before freezing.

Mocha Ice-Cream: Combine 1 cup hot water and 1 tablespoon instant coffee granules, stirring until granules dissolve. Let mixture cool slightly. Stir coffee mixture and 1 (5.5-ounce) can chocolate syrup into ice-cream mixture just before freezing.

Oreo Ice-Cream: Break up 15 Oreo cookies into small pieces. Stir into ice-cream mixture just before freezing.

Peach or Strawberry Ice-Cream: Pour 3-4 cups of fresh (or frozen) peaches/strawberries, sprinkled with sugar to taste, into ice-cream mixture in a blender. Blend before freezing.

Peanut Butter Ice-Cream: Stir ¾ cup chunky peanut butter into ice-cream mixture just before freezing. Serve ice-cream with chocolate syrup, if desired.

Peppermint Candy Ice-Cream: Substitute 2 teaspoons peppermint extract for vanilla. Add 2 cups hard pepppermint candies to ice-cream mixture before blending in a blender. For a crunchier taste, stir in an additional cup of crushed peppermints (or 1 cup of mini-chocolate chips) while ice-cream is still soft enough for stirring.

Pralines 'n Cream Ice-Cream: Add 2 cups of coarsely chopped candied pecans (page 94) to ice-cream mixture during freezing or after frozen, but while still soft.

Strawberry-Banana-Nut Ice-Cream: Stir 3 bananas, mashed; 1 pint strawberries, coarsely

Toffee Ice-Cream: Stir 1 (6-ounce) package Heath bar bits into ice-cream mixture just before freezing.

Editors' Notes: *To get the full benefit (especially the rich taste and creamy texture) of these recipes, do not use fat-free condensed milk or fat-free half-and-half. Reduced fat substitutes will work, but the taste and consistency are compromised (more with some flavors then others). These ice-cream recipes may be used for "make-your-own-sundae" parties where guests can make their own creations from an assortment of ice-creams and toppings. They may also be used to make ice-cream pies, parfaits, or to fill meringue shells.*

"Our Foods staff has taken the liberty of naming Maxine Pinson of Savannah the queen of ice-cream. We first planned to test her basic recipe and six variations. But we enjoyed all those so much that we picked three more flavors to test--then chose six more. We think you'll get carried away with this recipe, too." —*Southern Living*, August 1988

Just relaxing--a delightful B&B indulgence

"INNformation for INNgoers"

Topics Addressed in Q&A Section

Information about Q&A Section

All answers refer, specifically, to smaller bed and breakfast (approximately 2-8 rooms/ suites) or historic inns (approximately 9-25 rooms/suites). For easier reading, the term "inn" is used in reference to each, with clarifications made as needed. The questions are topically arranged, and the responses are divided into 2-4 parts (*only selected ones include quotes from innkeepers and "inn tales from inn trails"):

- **Brief response to question**

- **An "expanded" answer**

- ***Quotes from innkeepers in direct response to question**

- ***An "inn tale from the inn trail" relating to the issue**

Notes: *The B&Bs and historic inns shown in this section have been reviewed or recommended in The INNside Scoop B&B newsletter during the past few years. Each is one of The INNside Scoop's top-rated inns, based upon discerning criteria, and represents a sampling of the types of inns available. The photographs are randomly placed and do not, necessarily, relate to the juxtaposed questions being addressed. More information on these inns, including reviews on many, may be found at:*

www.innsidescoop.com

If you enjoy this "Innformation for Inngoers" section, you will love **INNside Scoop** (published in 2002)--especially the "inn tales"! For more information on this unique book, visit www.innsidescoop.com/is.htm or see page 221. A copy of the Table of Contents and Listing of Topics addressed in this book may also be viewed on the book's Web site. An autographed copy of the book may be ordered by calling **1-800-871-8977** or using the order form on page 222.

How I Got Hooked on B&Bs

Bill in front of Mrs. Hudspith's B&B in Edinburgh, Scotland.
The old photograph is faded, but the memories remain vivid.

I experienced my first B&B (bed and breakfast inn) during a trip to Ireland in 1971. My husband, Bill, and I were only there one night, but that was all it took for me to become a B&B aficionado forever. Now, over thirty years later, my enthusiasm for B&Bs continues.

During the summer of 1971, while Bill was an exchange student at Exeter University Law School in England, we had opportunities to visit Ireland, France, Italy, Scotland, Spain, Germany, Belgium, Holland, and Switzerland. Relying upon *Europe on Five Dollars A Day,* a travel guide published by Arthur Frommer for budget-conscious travelers, I developed our itinerary and made reservations at B&Bs in each country.

Of all the B&Bs we experienced, our most memorable was a small B&B in Edinburgh, Scotland. It was located on the street where *The Prime of Miss Jean Brodie,* by Muriel Spark, was filmed. Each morning, from our seat at the breakfast table, we watched a horse-drawn milk wagon making deliveries to homes along the cobble-stoned street in suburban Edinburgh.

The innkeeper, Mrs. Hudspith, was a wonderful Scottish lady who kept a fire blazing in the dining room and a table covered with freshly baked goodies. A pot of tea, warmed by a knitted teapot "cozy," stayed full. If it had not been for her kitchen guard dog, Bruce, I would have been tempted to sneak into her kitchen, after hours, for more of her homemade treats. Perhaps, that is why big-eyed Bruce was stationed in that particular spot--and he *never* left. I tried being nice to the mongrel, but he just glared and growled at me. I soon realized there was no use in trying to make a truce with Bruce. I thought it really annoying that this inhospitable Scot had to share the same name of my favorite cousin and our Scottish forebear, king Robert the Bruce It was sitting around Mrs. Hudspith's communal table, next to a warming fire after a day of touring in drizzly weather, that I became forever enamored with B&Bs. I love meeting new people and sharing stories. There is no better place for doing this than B&Bs.

How could I ever forget Mr. and Mrs. Willy from Vancouver, an octogenarian couple we met over breakfast at Mrs. Hudspith's? We stayed in touch for years. When our first child was born, Mrs. Willy crocheted a little pink cap and sent it to her. Each Christmas Bill and I received alluring Canadian calendars from the Willys, always accompanied by an invitation to visit them. I hoped we might be able to one day, but we never were. Our chance meeting was a "one moment in time" experience through which I feel my life was enriched.

Since that memorable trip in 1971, I have stayed at a variety of highly acclaimed resorts and world-class hotels, within the States and abroad. However, none of my fancy hotel experiences—from The Waldorf-Astoria in New York City to Rome, Italy's Hotel Excelsior—has provided me with the same cherished memories as those I have from favorite B&Bs. There is a major difference between simply *staying* somewhere and *experiencing* a place in its totality. I prefer the experiential, and I doubt my love for the wonderful world of B&Bs will wane.

Definitions and Distinctions

*The following definitions attempt to codify
what is presently being used in the field.
They are only approximations and will vary
by region or individual innkeeper.*

Reprinted, with permission, from PAII
(The Professional Association of Innkeepers International)
www.paii.org

Homestay, Host-Home

This type of establishment is an owner-occupied private home where the business of paying guests is secondary to its use as a private residence. The hosts are primarily interested in meeting new people and making some additional monies while continuing their present employment or retirement. Frequently located in residential areas, zoning or other government restrictions may prevent the use of signs, public advertising, etc. Usually between 1-3 rooms, these homes are often a member of, and usually inspected by a reservation service organization (RSO) but are rarely required to be licensed or inspected by local applicable governmental agencies. Breakfast is the only meal served. In some instances, it may be an unhosted apartment where breakfast is self-serve.

Bed and Breakfast

Formerly a single family dwelling usually in the 4-5-room range, this owner-occupied establishment has an equally mixed use as home and lodging with lodging superseding home more often than not. It is located in a legally zoned area and meets all the tax, fire, building and health requirements for this size and use of property. This establishment advertises publicly and can legally post a sign. Like the homestay or host home, because of its size, these B&Bs usually cannot support a family unit, so the B&B is often one partner's job and the other has outside income. Often the property is purchased specifically to be a B&B, but many are converted family homes. Reservations may be made directly with the property.

Bed and Breakfast Inn

(sometimes just called a Breakfast Inn)

Generally small, owner-operated businesses providing the primary financial support of the owner. Usually the owner lives on premises. The building's primary usage is for business. Inns advertise, have business licenses, produce their own brochures, comply with government ordinances, pay all appropriate taxes and post signs. Breakfast is the only meal served and only to overnight guests. The inn may host events such as weddings, small business meetings, etc. Room numbers range from 4-20 with a small, but increasing number up to 30. Reservations may be made directly with the property. Note: The distinction between a "B&B" and a "B&B inn" is not readily apparent, except with regard to building usage.

Country Inn

A business offering overnight lodging and meals where the owner is actively involved in daily operations, often living on site. These establishments are, in fact, B&B inns which serve at least one meal in addition to breakfast, and operate as "restaurants" as well as overnight lodging accommodations. Modified American plan (MAP) country inns serve dinner to overnight guests only, and the cost of dinner and breakfast is generally included in the room rate. A country inn with a full-service restaurant serves these additional meals to the general public. To be a country inn, a property does not have to be located in a rural area. Room numbers tend to range from 6 to 30. To understand bed-and-breakfast/country inn in the context of other properties that are confused with bed and breakfast, the following definitions are included:

Bed & Breakfast / Self-Contained Cottage

A detached building affording privacy and seclusion to guests, with owner providing minimal services. Breakfast is either delivered to the room, taken with others in a central dining room or placed prior to arrival (or upon daily cleaning) in the cottage kitchen facilities. Owner is usually available for questions, but generally guests choose this style of B&B when they want little help. Certain geographic regions see this type of lodging more than others. The light personal touch and memorable B&B decor further distinguish this genre from the vacation rental/condo.

Bed & Breakfast Hotel

These are 30+-room historic properties offering breakfast that can only be considered hotels. Only the historic structure, and perhaps some decorating components and breakfast provide the B&B feel.

Summary

Although all of the above categories view themselves as providing these below-listed characteristics, in reality, the larger the property--and particularly if the owner is not actively involved in daily operations and guest interaction--the property moves rapidly into the "hotel" perception in the minds of the traveller.

- Generous hospitality and personal attention to guests
- Architecturally interesting or historic structure
- Owner involvement in business
- Clean and comfortable ambiance and surroundings
- Individually decorated rooms

Burke Manor Inn
Gibsonville, NC

Basic Differences Between Inns and Traditional Accommodations

Q: What are advantages of staying at an inn?

A: The defining uniqueness is found in the distinctive characteristics each individual inn promises to provide. Inns are as different and individualistic as the innkeepers who run them, and they lack the sterility often associated with more traditional types of lodging. Personal service and guest pampering are trademarks of the inn industry. A stay at a bed and breakfast or historic inn is likely to be far more memorable than staying at a motel or hotel (many which now attach "inn" to their name).

Many inns are located within historic dwellings and provide an opportunity for personally experiencing fascinating homes in a way many would be unable to do otherwise. For individuals who are "people people," an inn provides an ideal setting for meeting and interacting with interesting people from all areas of our country and abroad. For those desiring privacy in their own zone, there are inns that are totally secluded. See "Why I'm Hooked on B&Bs" (p. 170).

One innkeeper presents a challenge to travelers: "Try going back to an inn for a second time and compare your treatment to what you receive when returning to a chain hotel." Another innkeeper relates, "I have started having more guests coming just to get gardening and/or decorating ideas. I know one caterer who frequents inns for recipe collecting."

Q: What are differences distinguishing the inn experience from a traditional stay at a chain hotel or motel, especially one which refers to itself as an "inn" and includes breakfast with the room?

A: The human factor and personal touches. Attention-to-detail. Having an opportunity to meet and interact with other guests. Memorable, home-cooked breakfasts—not pick-up items from the neighborhood donut shop or styrofoam coffee cups with stick stirrers.

Most inngoers can tell you the names of the innkeepers at their favorite inns long after their visit at the inn. Many times, they can name new friends or acquaintances met while there. I challenge anyone to tell you the name of a desk clerk at some non-descript motel or the name of a tuxedoed concierge at a swanky resort once the visit ends. How often have you met new friends or fascinating conversationalists while staying at a motel or hotel? As far as distinguishing between breakfasts at a traditional chain hotel/motel and the morning repast at an inn—well, there simply isn't a comparison. Breakfasts at inns vary as much as the inns serving them. The meal may be simple, plentiful, or a grand 3-course feast.

Q: Aren't inns primarily for the wealthy or socially elite?

A: Absolutely not. There is a bed and breakfast or an inn to suit every taste, budget, and personality. When you are ready to travel, spend some time checking out different inns on the Internet until you find one that appeals to you. Four good Web sites to begin with are:

www.innsidescoop.com
(less expansive than the others, but it includes a listing of outstanding inns in 30 states)
BedandBreakfast.com
TravelGuides.com
www.innmarketing.com/bbguide.htm
(lists numerous B&B links)

Victoria House Bed & Breakfast
Hampton, VA

Q: Are inns more or less expensive than traditional motels/hotels?

A: Many people think inns are cost-prohibitive. Not true. It is true that inns, especially larger historic inns, can be quite pricey. Inns located in popular tourist areas will always be more expensive than ones located in smaller towns or areas with fewer attractions, but some of these off-the-beaten-path inns are true gems. If you compare the price paid with the benefits received, you will discover inns are more affordable than you might suspect. Inns range from rural to urban, historic to modern, elegant to practical.

Expensive inns often offer special packages and a wide range of rooms at varying prices. Some offer special rates to civil servants. Even the big chains, including ones promising to *"leave the light on for you," aren't that cheap anymore. I consider the majority of inns fairly priced, considering their offerings and services. I feel some inns are worth more than they charge, while some are over-priced. If cost is a concern, clarify the details of what you will be receiving when you make your reservations.*

Somerset House
Talladega, AL

Q: Are there additional charges I might incur when staying at an inn?

A: My biggest pet peeve is when there is an unposted local charge for telephone calls made. Local calls, made from an inn, are usually free. Be aware of a possible parking expense if you are staying in a district where parking spaces are at a premium; you may need to purchase a city parking permit (for example, the cost is about $6 for 2 days in Savannah). Some inns provide them; others do not. Most inns do not charge for wine served at their wine reception or snacks/beverages in a guest refrigerator. Some do. If the inn has a staff, tipping is appreciated. Sometimes a service charge, for the room, is built into the rate. Just ask the inn-keeper, when the reservations are made, about any questions you may have.

Q: Are walk-ins accepted at inns like at traditional motels/hotels? Sometimes, when traveling, I like to remain flexible and plan my trip as I go.

A: Typically, hotels and motels have a staff member on duty round-the-clock. Most inns do not. Rooms are limited at inns and sometimes reserved far in advance. However, if a "walk-in" arrives during an inn's standard check-in time (usually between 3-7 p.m.) when there is availability, most innkeepers will accept the guest without a reservation.

Finding availability at an inn is much less likely on week-end nights or during a high-season period. Of course, cancellations can always occur at the last minute any day of the week or time of year. It is not advisable to start looking for an inn when you are tired of driving and ready to stop for the night. There are no billboards, along expressways, telling you where the next inn is located. Even if there were, just popping-in and finding a room available is less likely than at chain-type lodgings.

Not all innkeepers are keen on accepting guests without a reservation. One innkeeper ex-plains why: "Some inns promote having fresh flowers and/or fruit in a guest room upon the arrival of a guest. This is not always possible with a walk-in or a last minute reservation." Once again, it depends upon the policy of the inn and the innkeeper.

Q: Are most inns open year-round like traditional accommodations?

A: Yes. However, some inns close during seasons when few visitors come to their area, such as during the months of bitter cold in certain parts of New England. This information is usually posted on an inn's Web site. Larger inns (especially ones with a staff) are usually open year-round. Smaller ones usually close on Christmas Day so the innkeepers can spend time with their family. Sometimes a small inn closes for a month in January (or several weeks at another time during the year) so the innkeepers can have a break or make repairs (usually done in January). It varies with the inn.

Q: What did the majority of innkeepers do in "their other life?"

A: There is no stereotypical innkeeper any more than there is a stereotypical guest. They come from all walks of life, and their backgrounds run the gamut from A - Z.

Q: How about inngoers. Is there a profile for them?

A: They, too, come from all walks of life.

One innkeeper says, "Generally speaking, B&Bs attract guests who are more educated and sophisticated than average. Guests often find breakfast to be an interesting and entertaining experience."

The Importance of an Inn's Affiliation with a Professional Organization

Q: How important are ratings (such as AAA and Mobil) of inns?

A: With so many inns from which to choose, ratings help narrow the focus by letting one know the quality or service they may expect from a specific inn.

I have personally discovered unrated inns which I consider superior to some of the inns I have visited with a high rating from a prestigious organization. Even though Mobil and AAA are usually reliable in their ratings, just because an inn chooses not to be rated—for whatever reason—is not a reason to avoid going to it. Sometimes an excellent inn has not been in business long enough to undergo the inspection required for a rating.

A long-time innkeeper, owner of an established and successful inn, raises an important point. "It is important to remember that the ultimate test of an inn's quality is experiential. Owners of older establishments, under the same ownership for several generations, may not feel compelled to pay the fees of joining certain groups, even though they may meet or exceed the criteria of the various standards of the inspection." Another experienced innkeeper states, "Many of their requirements are not necessary. In some cases, they can actually detract from an inn's uniqueness."

Q: How important is an inn's affiliation with a professional inn group, and what are some of these established organizations an inngoer should know about?

A: Very important. Affiliation with established associations provides assurance to the inngoer that certain basics (such as cleanliness, food codes, and safety) have been met and approved. But, keep in mind, the quality of an inn is not a prerequisite for becoming a member of state bed and breakfast associations, PAII (Professional Association of Innkeepers International), or similar type organizations.

Most state associations set standards that must be met, including periodic inspections. Inclusion in a bed and breakfast directory (online or in most travel guides, unless stated otherwise) requires nothing more than payment for inclusion. Some private groups are more exclusive than others and issue invitations (with a hefty fee) for membership.

Amenities and Services

Q: What is the difference between amenities and services at an inn?

A: In the May 2002 edition of Innkeeping, published by The Professional Association of Innkeepers International (PAII), amenities and services are addressed. "Some innkeepers use a limited definition of amenities that includes only items guests can carry away with them: fragrant soap, wrapped in the inn's private label, would be an amenity; the Jacuzzi in the room would not. At the other end of the spectrum, some innkeepers—in keeping with AAA categorization—might label room décor, such as elegant draperies or marble bath counters, amenities. Services, as well as objects, can be amenities."

Q: What types of amenities may I expect at an inn?

A: The extent of amenities varies with the inn and may be restricted to the basics or exceed the bounds of one's imagination. Amenities at an inn may include: clock radios, televisions/VCRs, CD players (sometimes with CDs), terry cloth robes (sometimes slippers), an array of toiletries (shampoo, conditioner, body lotion, make-up remover cloths, etc.), hairdryers, an iron and ironing board, working fireplace, whirlpool tub, European showers, heated bathroom floors, heated towel racks. The list continues ad infinitum.

One creative innkeeper tucks fresh lilac into a roll of lavendar-colored netting, tied on the ends with lavendar satin ribbon, between the pillows at turn-down. She sprays the bed linens, when ironing them, with a lavendar spritz made with vodka.

Safety Issues

Q: Is it safe for a woman, traveling alone, to stay at an inn?

A: Very. It is probably the safest place a woman traveling alone can stay.

As a travel writer, I often travel alone when reviewing inns. I have never experienced an inn where I felt safety was an issue of concern.

Q: Why are some B&Bs so picky about having the entrance doors always locked?

A: For the same reason most people prefer to have their entrance doors locked at home. The B&Bs are the homes of most innkeepers, and homeowners want to know their property is secure. Innkeepers have the additional responsibility (and liability) of having guests to look out for, as well as their own belongings.

Children and Pets

Bonnie Castle
Grantville, GA

Q: Are B&Bs and inns appropriate for children?

A: Most are not, even though they may be accepted at a certain age. Children are much happier at a family-oriented type of lodging. Inns do not cater to children, and sometimes their behavior causes discontent with other guests.

A gourmet breakfast, along with interaction with other adult guests, can be ruined by a crying baby or an ill-mannered child. Many couples go to an inn to get a reprieve from children.

One innkeeper says, "I don't think a couple on honeymoon would appreciate toddlers running around on hardwood floors above their honeymoon suite. Older children often find breakfast conversation, an integral part of the B&B experience, to be boring."

Q: Do B&Bs object to guests bringing pets to stay in their room with them?

A: Most inns do not permit pets. Inns allowing pets usually have a notice posted on their Web site. Some inns offer barns for equestrian travelers who travel with their horse(s) in tow. As always, whenever in question, just ask. But, do not expect most inns to accept furry friends.

Special Needs

Q: Are most inns set up for guests who are physically challenged in some way?

A: More and more inns are offering special accommodations, always at ground level, for physically challenged guests. If there is a possibility you might encounter a problem at the inn, because of a physical situation, be sure to discuss it with the innkeeper when you call to inquire or make a reservation. They will be able to provide the assurance you need or help you find another place better suited for your particular needs.

Inn tale: When it is time to shower, make sure you are not wider than the stall. One inn guest got stuck in a shower stall in Georgia and couldn't get out. He was traveling with a friend, who had a room across the hall. When his friend heard the yelp for help, he performed a successful rescue operation--with the help of a bar of slippery soap and some hefty tugging.

Business & Corporate Travel

The Duke Mansion
Charlotte, NC

Q: Do inns cater to business and corporate travelers?

A: Most definitely. Some have mini-suites, complete with a kitchen, for regulars who stay a week or more at a time (usually at a lower rate). Inns catering to business travelers customarily offer fax and copier services, private telephone lines, and an early breakfast option. Some even have a mini-office set up for business guests.

Most innkeepers do not object to faxes being sent to their guests within reason. Sending lengthy documents is not acceptable. One innkeeper tells the story of a thousand page deposition faxed to an attorney staying at their inn. Not to be done!

Q: Do inns accept long-termers?

A: Some inns prefer long-termers, especially individuals in the military. Individuals training or relocating to the area are also welcomed while waiting for housing to become available. Long-termers are usually given discounted rates and sometimes given special privileges (i.e., use of the laundry facilities). In exchange for the lower rate, breakfast and daily clean-up may not be included.

Inn tale: I have an innkeeper friend who caters to long-termers, especially military personnel. Whenever she gets a new military guest, she welcomes them by placing a special alarm clock under their bed and setting it to activate the next morning. The clock is a replica of a drill sergeant, and it "activates" by the drill sergeant playing a bugle and yelling, "Get up!" Get Up! Good morning." Imagine the surprise of a guest hearing that first thing in the morning and then finding that loud-mouthed, bossy sergeant under their bed!

Different Types of Inns

Q: Does B&B always stand for "Bed & Breakfast" in the travel industry?

A: "Bed and Breakfast" is what B&B traditionally refers to in the travel industry. However, all kinds of adaptations have evolved: Bed & Biscuits, Bed & Bagel, Bed & Basket, Barn & Breakfast, Bed & Boat. There is one inn named "Bed, No Breakfast."

Inn Tale: A typographical blooper once advertised a unique "Bed & Broad." One inn reports that after a man reserved a room for a night (in a state where prostitution is legal), he asked the innkeeper, in all seriousness: "Does a girl come with the room?"

Q: What is considered a traditional B&B and what characterizes traditional innkeepers?

A: A long-time innkeeper verbalizes the basic framework upon which a "traditional" B&B, operated by traditional innkeepers, is recognized. She states: "At a traditional B&B, guests are treated more like house guests or personal friends than a boarder. The atmosphere experienced and hospitality received is more like one would find at the home of a favorite friend or relative. The majority of innkeepers at traditional inns are seasoned in the art of hosting, and their primary concern is the comfort and enjoyment of their guests. These innkeepers are usually accessible and guest-oriented. Initially, traditional B&Bs refrained from putting TVs and telephones in guest rooms to protect guests from interruptions of the outside world during a getaway. However, that trend is changing. More and more B&Bs now have telephones or TVs (even VCRs) in their guest rooms, especially the larger ones."

Sylvan Falls Mill B&B
Rabun Gap, GA

Selecting an Inn

Q: How do I know what an innkeeper considers "nice" are the same things I consider nice?

A: You don't. Asking an innkeeper if their inn is "nice" is kind of like someone asking if you think your own child is "cute." Of course, an innkeeper thinks their inn is nice. And, even if is not quite up to the standards they wish it were, I do not think an innkeeper is likely to say, "Well, not really..."

We each have our own mental image of what adjectives depict. What I may consider nice, cozy, elegant, luxurious, or gourmet may not be in sync with an innkeeper's concept of these words at all. Even guests will differ on the accuracy of adjectives applied to an inn. Concepts are formed by one's personal frame-of-reference and life experience--it does not mean one is right and the other is wrong.

Q: I have found that inns do not always measure up to the glorious images they portray in their brochures or on theirWeb sites. How can I know whether what I see in print (or online) is what I'll find on-site?

A: Not finding on-site what is promoted online (or in a slick, glitzy brochure) is my greatest pet-peeve of the industry. Of course, this is not something limited to B&Bs or inns. I prefer selecting an inn whose Web site or brochure shows as many photographs as possible (guest rooms, dining area, common areas, outside areas). I also like to have an idea of the neighborhood. Virtual tours are excellent as they provides 360 degree coverage of the rooms and surrounding area outside. If an inn's Web site offers one, take advantage of it.

If an area is blatantly absent, my radar starts beeping. For example, if there are beautiful photographs of the common areas, but none of the guest quarters--or vice versa. Of course, there are all sort of techniques for improving the appearance of a photograph. Pay attention to the furnishings and decor, if that is something important to you. Also, I find innkeepers who take care to provide a high-quality, informative Web site usually run a high-quality inn. Be wary of inns using superlatives and claims with nothing to back them up.

Inn tale: I will never forget the time I went to an inn proclaiming (online and in the state B&B directory) that they had the *best* breakfast in the state. Says who? Apparently, the innkeeper had not visited some of the stellar inns, with gourmet fare, in that state that I have had the opportunity of experiencing. The same inn had a sign, in front of their inn, stating their yard was the "yard of the month"--in small letters, beneath this announcement, it stated: "proclaimed by the owner." I find such claims misleading and deceptive, not cute or amusing.

Getting the Best Rates

Q: Do inns offer seasonal rates?

A: This is usually dependent upon the location of the inn and the degree of tourism in the area at specific times of the year.

It is almost impossible to get a room (unless reserved a year in advance or more) in Savannah for the green week of Savannah's annual St. Patrick's Day festivities. However, incredibly low rates (in comparison to the usual rates) are often offered at different Savannah inns during the slower months of January and February. Look on the Web sites of inns for specials offered, or call and inquire if seasonal rates are not noted on the inn's Web site.

Q: Can I get a room for less if I am not interested in breakfast or clean-up service?

A: I have only been to a few inns willing to reduce the rate if you are not interested in the daily clean-up service. This option is primarily restricted to long-termers. Of course, you may always ask—but please respect the policy the innkeepers have decided upon, whatever it may be.

Contacting an Inn

Zero Water Street B&B
Charleston, SC

Q: Why is a toll-free and a regular telephone number often listed for an inn?

A: A toll-free number is established specifically for making inquiries, reservations, or cancellations. Most innkeepers do not object to calls being made on their toll-free line to let them know you are arriving later or earlier than originally scheduled.

It is not acceptable to leave an inn's toll-free number with your children, a baby-sitter, or anyone else for the purpose of contacting you during your stay at the inn. Neither is it acceptable for a personal message or greeting to be delivered to you via an inn's toll-free line.

Q: When is the best time to call an inn?

A: The best time to call smaller inns is between 10 a.m. and 5 p.m. local time (never during the time breakfast is being prepared/served or late at night). Larger inns, with a staff on duty, may receive calls until 10 p.m—especially in vacation cities. Restrain from becoming annoyed if an answering machine picks up instead of a real, live person—especially if the inn is small and does not have someone to mind the phone round-the-clock. For most innkeepers of small inns, a wireless phone is like an extra appendage. But they cannot be available to answer the phone at all times. They do have shopping to do and personal business to tend. When calling an inn outside your locale, be aware of the time zone.

If a potential guest from the East Coast calls an inn on the West Coast at 8 a.m., the phone will be ringing out there before the rooster crows. See if you can find the information you need on the inn's Web site. Almost all inns have one now. Actually, if I can't see an inn online, I seldom consider it--which is why I feel so strongly about online honesty in true representation of an inn.

Q: Are inns willing to rent out their entire facility to a group?

A: Most inns (small B&Bs as well as larger ones) often rent out their entire facility to wedding parties or private groups.

Because of the home-like atmosphere of B&Bs, they provide an attractive option for a variety of private functions

Making, Securing, and Canceling Reservations

Inn at Folkston
Folkston, GA

Q: Do most inns offer online availability and online reservations for guests?

A: More inns are offering online availability and online reservations. Some inns provide an online room chart indicating which rooms are available on which dates. This service provides a valuable convenience for both inngoer and innkeeper, in addition to minimizing telephone calls and costs. Online availability shows which rooms are available, at that moment, so online reservations may be made and secured.

A disadvantage of online reservations is that it eliminates valuable discourse between an innkeeper and a potential guest. Engaging in a one-on-one conversation, with an innkeeper, allows the inngoer to get a feel for an innkeeper's manner and style. This is important since an inn is, in essence, a reflection of the innkeeper who manages it. Smaller B&Bs are likely to require a phone call follow-up so the innkeeper can also get a feel for the type of inn the guest is seeking. This way, the guest is more likely to get the property best suited for specific desires and needs.

An innkeeper says, "We update our online availability manually, and so it may not always be current. If *no availability* shows, it is best to call the inn just to double-check for accuracy."

Q: Do inns require reservations to be guaranteed?

A: The majority of inns do require reservations to be secured by a credit card and usually have their policy stated on its Web site or brochure.

Many inns require an advance deposit. Be sure to find out if they are just holding your credit card number or actually charging your card. Smaller B&Bs (and even some medium-sized historic inns) are not set up to accept credit cards and require payment with cash or check. The standard requirement is full payment for one night; however, it may be more for extended stays, during a "high season," and times of special events.

Q: What if I need to cancel my reservations at an inn?

A: If the need for cancellation arises, call the innkeeper as soon as possible. Most innkeepers are willing to accommodate whenever they can, but revenue from the renting of rooms is what keeps them in business. Cancellation policies vary, but most inns have theirs posted on their Web site and must adhere to them. Sometimes an inn will provide you a gift certificate (usually valid for one year) to use when you can come.

Smaller inns often fill up far in advance during special seasons or local events. When there is a last-minute cancellation, the room is more difficult to fill since many would not expect the inn to have an opening. Above all, respect the inn's cancellation policy, and most innkeepers will work with you in working out arrangements mutually satisfactory.

Packing for an Inn Stay

Q: Is there any set dress code for guests staying at inns?

A: No. Most guests (and innkeepers) dress according to the "2-C" code: casual and comfortable, even at the more formal inns. If you see someone dressed up, they are probably a business traveler, on the way to an appointment, or someone going to a dress-up affair.

If the inn has a swimming pool or a hot tub, they probably provide terry cloth robes (usually mentioned on the Web site). But, just in case they do not, take a cover-up along. The common areas of an inn are no place to strut your stuff--not even if it the inn is beachside.

Arriving at an Inn

Q: Is there a procedure I should follow if I need to arrive before or after regular check-in times?

A: This is an easy question to answer. You simply do the same as you would want an expected personal guest to do if visiting in your home. *You call* and let the innkeeper know when you will be arriving, and you call again if that changes. To do otherwise is rude. Read my lips on this one: to arrive early or late, without calling, is rude, rude, rude.

When you call to let the innkeeper know you are running late (or to ask if you may arrive earlier than originally scheduled), a courteous and sincere "I hope this will not be an inconvenience to you" is always appreciated. I don't know about you, but I really get annoyed when someone doesn't show up, within a reasonable time frame, when they tell me they will be arriving. Innkeepers are no different. The innkeepers of smaller inns often have no outside help, and it is thoughtless to keep a busy innkeeper waiting for hours on end for a late arrival. Sometimes they arrange their schedules specifically for the arrival of a guests. It is equally ill-mannered to arrive hours in advance of the agreed-upon time of arrival. Most innkeepers, I know, are caring individuals who worry when guests have not shown up or called hours after they are expected. I hear more complaints about early and late arrivals, from innkeepers, than all others combined. The bottom line: don't do it—not even to "just drop your bags off and use the bathroom."

Q: When I arrive at an inn, do I ring the doorbell or just walk on in?

A: Depends on the inn's size and location. B&Bs usually keep their entrance door locked. There may be a note indicating whether you should knock, ring the bell, or go to another entrance. Larger inns, with a staff member seated within viewing distance of the door, often have the door unlocked so guests may let themselves in.

Some inns have a telephone on the porch so the innkeeper may be called when you arrive. One of my favorite inns has an ornamental iron gate at the estate's entrance. Guests are given the code before arrival. After keying it in, the gate swings open--to paradise!

Q: If I am interested in staying at an inn, but do not have reservations, may I just let myself in for a peek-about?

A: No siree--never! Remember, B&Bs are also private homes. Would you want someone to just walk into your home for a little "peek-about"?

Inn tale: One innkeeper retired from innkeeping after a father and his child walked in on her taking a bath in the private quarters of her B&B.

Q: If I see an inn I would like to stay at, but no one is there to check me in, may I just select a room and check myself in?

A: If I had not heard a story about someone who actually did this, I would consider the question too preposterous to dignify with a response which, of course, is an emphatic "no."

Inn tale: An innkeeper, a lady who has a secluded mountain inn and never locks the entrance doors during the day, returned home to find a guest who had taken the liberty of checking himself in. Walking in, with a bag full of groceries, she was greeted by a man wearing an inn robe and sipping a glass of sherry.

Q: Will I have to listen to the history of an inn, or go on a grand tour of rooms and grounds, before being shown to my quarters?

A: "Orientation time" varies from inn-to-inn, and it is a requirement of some organizations to which inns may belong. However, most innkeepers realize that guests—especially those who have travelled a long distance—are anxious to be shown their room and get situated. Often an innkeeper will ask if you'd like to see the inn "now" or "later." Usually, "later" is the wiser answer. On warm or cool days, an innkeeper may offer you something hot or cold to drink upon your arrival. And, for heaven's sake, if you need to use the restroom upon arriving, ask where it is! You can be polite and attentive to inn stuff afterwards. First things first!

The Gragg House
Boone, NC

Q: What if I do not like my accommodations when I first see them?

A: Most innkeepers are not happy if their guests are not happy. If you are displeased with your room, ask the innkeeper if there is another room available that you may have instead. Be prepared to pay more if it is an upgrade. If a legitimate problem develops in your room (plumbing, heating, etc.) that is beyond your control and which cannot be corrected within a timely period, you are entitled to another room, if available, at no extra charge.

Q: If I feel I have legitimate complaints about the inn or the innkeepers, is there someone I can register my concerns with?

A: Check the inn's Web site or brochure to see if the inn is affiliated with a state organization or PAII. If so, contact one of these groups about the problem. If you would like to address the innkeepers directly, refrain from addressing your grievance in front of other guests.

Q: When do I pay for my room at an inn?

A: This varies with the personal preference of the innkeeper. Some innkeepers prefer getting "the unpleasantries" over and done with at the beginning; others prefer waiting until check-out time, especially if they anticipate additional charges being added to your account.

Bathrooms at B&Bs

Q: I stayed in B&Bs in Europe, and I often had to share a bath with other guests. I do not like sharing a bath with strangers, and so I do not go to inns anymore.

A: Almost all American inns have private baths for *each* of their guest rooms--and I would say 98% of them are adjacent to the bedroom. If a bath is shared, it is usually located between two rooms rented by guests traveling together. An inn's Web site and brochure indicate whether its accommodations include a private bath or not.

Occasionally, a room has a private bath, but it is located across the hall. When this is the case, a robe is usually provided for the guest, and a sign is posted that the bath is a private one (reserved for guests staying in a particular room). In older structures, finding a way to provide an adjacent bath, for each guest room, often provides a challenge--one which sometimes escapes a satisfactory solution.

Q: Is it okay to use bubble bath in an inn's whirlpool tubs?

A: It depends on the individual model. Whirlpool tubs vary in operation and range of capability. Instructions are often posted in the bathroom. If you have any questions about its use, check with the innkeeper prior to using it.

Q: What if you can't figure out how to operate the tub? Some are so fancy and high-tech!

A: Same answer as above.

Inn Tale: The only time I have ever had to call an innkeeper, after hours, was when I could not figure out how to turn off an ultra-modern soaking tub. It required more computer knowledge, to operate its digital keypad, than I have--and I work with computers all the time.

Q: Are the toiletries sitting out for me to keep?

A: The individual (not the pint-sized) containers are provided for your convenience, and you may certainly take whatever you do not use with you. But, please, leave the extra rolls of toilet paper and tissue at the inn. You only pay for your needs while at the inn.

Gratuities and Additional Charges

Q: Are there any other charges I might incur while staying at an inn?

A: Not usually. If there are, it is usually at the larger inns. If you feel there might be, just ask when you make reservations if there are additional costs involved (such as a service charge).

If parking is a problem in the area of the inn, you may be required to purchase a parking permit in order to park on the street. Some inns provide these for their guests at no charge. But the parking permit is usually far less than the charge would be for parking in a hotel garage.

If you need to make local calls or need to go online, check to see if local calls are free. Typically, there is an information book in each guest room at an inn with basic information. If there is a charge, it will probably be noted in this book. I have never stayed at a B&B where there is a charge for local calls. However, sometimes larger inns charge up to 75 cents per local call. This is not customary at an inn presenting itself as a B&B--a fact I always make a point to bring to the management's attention.

Q: Is there a standard tipping policy at inns?

A: Just as each B&B is different, so is the question of tipping. Whether you stay in a B&B, inn, motel, or hotel, it is courtesy to leave $1 to $5 per night for the housekeepers; I usually leave the money on the dresser. The exact amount varies with the length of the stay, the price of the property, the size of the room, and the services rendered. If the B&B is quite small, and the owners do the housekeeping themselves, no tip is necessary. Since many people are unaware of this practice, many innkeepers have taken to leaving tipping envelopes as a gentle re-minder to guests, although there is no obligation to leave anything, especially if the house-keeping is not up to par. Personally, we don't much care for the practice, and would prefer a no-tipping policy, with the housekeepers paid a good wage, but recognize that that's not always possible. If you're not sure, it's always okay to ask. Last but not least, remember that inns which include accommodations, breakfast, and dinner in the rates typically add a 15% service fee to the entire amount. (*Reprinted by permission of Sandra W. Soule, Editor, BedandBreakfast.com*)

Inn at Covered Bridge Green
Arlington, VT

Breakfast Time at Inns

Q: When staying at a B&B, am I expected to eat at the same table and socialize with other guests?

A: Some inns have individual tables where a single traveler or a couple may eat alone. This is especially true at the larger historic inns. But, at a typical B&B, expect to share breakfast at a table of strangers who, chances are, will become friends before the meal is over.

No innkeeper (I hope!) is going to make you talk to anyone else or start the day off with any of those aggravating little "ice-breaker, talk-maker" games. But, if you are at a communal table, having breakfasts with other guests, it is customary and polite to at least say "howdy." Newspapers are not read at the table to the exclusion of other guests. As a rule, I have found guests at inns to be friendly folk whose company I thoroughly enjoy.

Q: What kind of food is served for breakfast at inns? Is the menu comparable throughout the week, or does it vary on the week-ends?

A: Everything imaginable: simple, Continental, deluxe, a full country breakfast, a gourmet breakfast, a 3-course feast (which usually begins with a fruit dish, followed by a breakfast entrée, and finished off with something sweet). Larger inns sometimes offer a menu, but this is unusual. A few inns provide a menu selection, the night before, from which breakfast selections may be made. Most innkeepers will ask, sometimes when the reservations are made, about food allergies or restrictions (dietary, religious, or other). Some innkeepers post the breakfast menu in a creative manner.

Q: What time is breakfast served?

A: It varies with the inn. Some innkeepers just have one seating, but most offer a time span.

Most innkeepers are willing to accommodate their guests however they can. If a guest has an early flight or an early business meeting, an early breakfast can often be arranged.

Q: When traveling, I enjoy meeting important people who are intelligent and in my socio-economic class. I don't hobnob or eat with just anyone. Will I be able to meet people like me at inns?

A: I sincerely hope not—and I particularly hope I never end up across the table from you. If you are primarily interested in picking up new names to drop (or impressing others with your importance), it would behoove you to seek your ilk elsewhere.

Even though inngoers include celebrities and high-profile individuals, around the breakfast table everyone is just "Jane" or "Joe."

Q: I am accustomed to saying a blessing at breakfast. Are blessings said at the breakfast table of most inns?

A: A blessing is not customarily said at an inn's communal breakfast table. However, saying grace is an individual choice. A guest may bow his head and bless his food, without a comment to anyone but the one to whom thanks are being offered.

Q: When eating at a communal table, must I wait until everyone is seated before I may begin eating?

A: Absolutely not. Breakfast, at an inn, is not like a seated dinner or a formal banquet. For the most part, the modus operandi at inns is very laid-back and amazingly casual—much more than most people realize or anticipate.

Q: Do innkeepers usually join their guests at breakfast time.

A: Some do, but most do not.

Q: If I finish eating, before the other guests, may I excuse myself and leave the table.

A: Certainly.

Q: When I first get up in the morning, I don't like to talk. When I am traveling alone, I prefer eating alone. Will an innkeeper feel obligated to sit and "keep me company," during breakfast, if I am the only guest at the inn?

A: This might happen occasionally, but not usually. For one thing, innkeepers have a full agenda in the morning. Sometimes an innkeeper will ask if you would like for them to sit with you. If you prefer eating alone, just say so in a courteous manner.

Q: Is it necessary to get dressed for breakfast at an inn?

A: Even though you may feel quite at home at an inn, especially a smaller B&B, it is not appropriate to show up for breakfast in your nightie, robe, stocking feet, or barefoot. Even though bare feet are not acceptable, bare heads (no baseball caps or curlers, please) are preferred. Other than that, as long as you are dressed decently, almost anything goes. There is no right or wrong dress code at inns, and most people dress casually. I do not see a problem sauntering down, for a cup of early morning coffee, in a cover-all robe.

One innkeeper says, "the tone of an inn sets the stage for appropriate dress."

Inn at Wintersun
Fairview, NC

Q: I was not brought up with a "silver spoon" in my mouth or exposed to the finer things in life until I was an adult. I worry about looking uncouth when I am uncertain about the correct silverware to use or other dining etiquette.

A: Not to worry! If it would make you feel better, refer to the Table Manners section on pages 204-205. The best thing to do, when uncertain about which utensil to use, is to look and see which one someone else is using. Of course, they may not know either and might be waiting to see what you do!

Some inns set formal breakfast tables with fine crystal and sterling silver. Others serve breakfast down-home style. If you should slip up and make a faux pas, don't worry about it. You'll probably never see any of the folks at your table again anyhow.

Q: If I am engaged in a conversation with other guests after finishing eating, does the innkeeper expect us to move to another area?

A: Most innkeepers are delighted when they see guests enjoying each other's company and establishing new friendships. However, I have heard some innkeepers comment that they would prefer guests visiting elsewhere so breakfast clean-up can be completed.

If uncertain, ask the innkeeper. If an innkeeper insists that you continue visiting at the table, then feel free to do so. However, if you sense the innkeeper would really like for you to visit elsewhere, it would be best to find another spot. There are usually a number of places, at an inn, where guests may talk and visit. At more formal inns, fine china is used at breakfast time and must be washed by hand. This is time consuming, and innkeepers are usually anxious to clear the table so they can move onto to the next item on their daily agenda.

Q: Is it okay for request an inn recipe?

A: Most innkeepers are happy to share their recipes. Some inns have even compiled cookbooks, with favorite recipes of their guests, which they sell at their inn.

Q: Are meals other than breakfast offered at inns?

A: Not often, but sometimes. Some inns, especially larger ones, may offer a prix fixe dinner. Inns sometimes offer to prepare dinner, with advance notice, especially when local restaurants are limited or not available. However, the food offered is usually limited. If you are interested in having all meals available, a "country inn" or an inn resort is more in line with what you are seeking.

Q: My husband and I are newlyweds and very much in love. Sometimes we just have trouble keeping our hands off each other! Are other guests going to be offended by any show of affection between us?

A: A public show-of-affection, within moderation, should never be offensive to anyone. If it is, they are probably just jealous! Holding hands conveys connectivity and tenderness between two people. However, the undercover stuff should be done under cover.

At the Inn Alone

Q: If I am at an inn alone and the phone rings, should I answer it?

A: Not unless the innkeeper has requested that you do so.

Q: If I am at the inn alone and someone comes to the door, should I let them in?

A: Unless it is another guest, who you know is staying at the inn, you should *not* let anyone in.

Q: If I am alone at an inn before going to bed, should I turn off all the lights?

A: No. Some inns have their lights on timers. Smaller inns usually have a procedure for turning off lites before retiring. For insurance and safety purposes, certain lights are left on so guests can go and come comfortably.

Q: I love exploring new places—opening closed doors and looking into the cubby holes. Is this okay to do while staying at an inn?

A: If there are closed doors, with or without privacy signs, do *not* open them. They are closed for a reason.

Q: If I need something from the kitchen when the innkeeper is not around, is it permissible to go in and get it?

A: No, not unless the innkeeper has, specifically, invited you to do so. Some state health department regulations forbid guests from entering an inn's kitchen. If you see a "private" sign on the kitchen door, interpret it as a polite way of saying: "Stay out."

Schell Haus
Pickens, SC

Telephones, Fax Machines, and Internet Access

Q: My work requires that I travel with a laptop and have online access. Is this available at most inns?

A: The majority of inns now have a telephone in each guest room, and the larger ones often have private guest lines (sometimes with an answering machine or voice mail). More and more inns are now providing modems for laptop computers in guest rooms.

Smaller inns are less likely to have telephones in guest rooms. Those that do not have phones in guest rooms usually have a guest phone (set up in a private area) or a cordless phone that can be taken into one's room. If there is a telephone in your room, make sure that using it for Internet access will not interfere with business calls to the inn or disable other guests from using the phone. When a telephone line is shared by guests, an innkeeper will sometimes post "Internet guidelines" for usage. You will also need to check to see if a "9," needs to be dialed in order to get an outside line.

Q: Should I give the inn's main telephone number as a number where I can be reached while staying there?

A: Calling a guest on a business line should be reserved, primarily, for emergency calls. If you anticipate receiving calls during a visit at an inn and do not have a cell phone of your own, ask the innkeeper (before arriving) how you may be contacted. If you will have a private line in your room, the innkeeper can give the number to you in advance.

Smoking, Alcoholic Beverages, Illegal Drugs

Q: Do most B&Bs have a no-smoking policy?

A: Yes, and the no-smoking policy is adhered to and enforced. No exceptions. Some innkeepers require guests to sign a statement saying they understand the no-smoking policy of the inn and agree that they (and members of their party) will abide by it. The statement forewarns guests that if they do smoke inside, a hefty fine (usually $200-$500) is added to their bill for the extra cleaning required. An innkeeper may also ask a guest, who violates the no-smoking policy, to leave the premises immediately without a refund.

Inn Tale: A sign at one inn reads: "If we see you smoking, we'll assume you are on fire and will take appropriate action."

Q: Is taking a cooler, filled with iced-down beer, to an inn acceptable?

A: Save the beer-filled coolers for a tail-gate event or for week-ends at Motel 6. Walking through a family-run B&B or an elegant historic inn, carrying a cooler, is tacky. If you are staying in a stand-alone cottage, on the premises of an inn, then it is okay.

What might not be acceptable in one situation might be perfectly acceptable in another.

One innkeeper says: "I've never objected to coolers in my guest rooms. However, guests are usually considerate enough to ask first. We cater to nature-based tourism, and our guests often need coolers for their excursions." Another says, it doesn't bother us since a lot of guests don't want to go out to dinner, but I wouldn't show up carrying a cooler instead of a suitcase."

Q: Is there a policy concerning the use of alcoholic beverages at inns?

A: The use of alcoholic beverages varies with the inn and the legalities of the area where the inn is located. Many inns offer wine (at an afternoon wine reception) and/or cordials at turn-down. However, the availability of hard liquor at inns is not customary. Again, this question/answer section is referring, specifically, to smaller B&Bs or historic inns, not country inns.

Q: I don't care about little afternoon teas or wine receptions. When 5 o'clock comes, I want a real drink. Will I be able to get the ice and set-up I need at an inn?

A: Listen up, sweetheart. If you want a real drink, then be real sure you can handle it without becoming loud or offensive to other guests. This applies, of course, to any drinking. Innkeepers are happy to provide ice and often have ice-buckets available that you may take to your room. Loud and rowdy partying, at an inn, is not tolerated. An inn is not a tavern.

Q: Can I smoke pot, in my room, while at a remote inn off-the-beaten path?

A: The use of illegal drugs is never acceptable at an inn, no matter how remote it might be. Don't even think about it.

Inn Tale: One guest decided to give it a try, but it didn't work. The innkeeper was also a county police officer and picked up the odor right away.

Checking Out and Settling Up

Inn at Warner Hall
Gloucester, VA

Q: What is the standard check-out time at B&Bs?

A: The check-out time at most B&Bs is 11 a.m., and it is important that guests check-out on time. Preparing rooms for the next guests takes time, especially when the innkeepers do not have outside help.

Q: If I need to extend my check-out time by an hour or two, is that a problem at a B&B?

A: Yes, it usually is a problem for the reason given above. However, if it is mid-week and you know new guests are not expected that day, you might be able to extend your stay by an hour.

Q: Do I pay my bill when I am ready to check-out?

A: The bill is usually paid at check out. However, some inns prefer handling the financial part at check-in. It depends on the policy of the inn.

Q: If I decide that I would like to extend my stay at an inn for one or more days, is there any procedure that needs to be followed for an extension? Would it be inappropriate to ask to move into another room?

A: Just let the innkeeper know, as soon as possible, that you are interested in staying over. If there is availability, there should be no problem. If you decide to stay over and would like to move into another room, most innkeepers will not mind as long as the one you want is available. Of course, if your new room costs more than your original one, you will be expected to pay the difference (unless you are able to work out the difference due to your extended stay).

Barrier Island Bed and Breakfast
St. Augustine, FL

Weddings, Receptions, and Honeymooning at Inns

Q: What is the appeal of having a wedding or reception at a B&B, and what are things I need to be aware of when planning an inn wedding or reception?

A: Inns are favorite spots for weddings and receptions because of the elegant facilities, picturesque settings, and attention-to-detail they offer. Inns specializing in weddings and receptions may offer special wedding packages (including catering and set-up). Most inns, specializing in weddings and receptions, are also able to suggest photographers, florists, catering services, music accompaniment, etc. Sometimes suppliers will work harder to please an innkeeper, than an individual, since they know an innkeeper will provide repeat business. Expect to pay an extra charge for outside services, a percentage to the innkeeper who makes the contacts and arrangements, and (possibly) a damages deposit.

If an inn is small, the wedding party (usually in range of 10 or more) may be required to rent the entire inn for a minimum of 2 nights.

Q: When weddings and/or wedding receptions are held at a B&B, are rooms also rented to individuals not connected with or attending the wedding?

A: Some inns require the hosting group to pay a flat fee (which covers booking the entire inn), before they agree to having a wedding reception at their inn. Other inns will continue renting rooms to guests not connected with the wedding. A wedding reception is, in essence, a big party which often becomes disruptive for other guests—especially when the reception is held after 8 p.m. It is unfair to the non-wedding guests when they are not free to use the facilities and grounds for which they pay.

Some inns will not agree to hosting wedding parties, even though they have the facilities and space. The noise factor is usually the reason why. They do not want their clientele deprived of the peace and quiet they are paying to receive.

Q: Do most inns have a honeymoon suite or a separate cottage catering to honeymooners?

A: Most of the larger inns do have a honeymoon suite or a separate cottage designed for honeymooners. However, even the smaller B&Bs usually have a room (or suite) they refer to as their "honeymoon suite."

Q: I would like to spend my honeymoon at a B&B, but I don't want to eat breakfast with a table of grinning "well-wishers."

A: Innkeepers are respectful of the privacy desired by newlyweds, and they are willing to accommodate their wishes however possible. If you would like to have breakfast alone, ask if you may eat at a separate table (perhaps in another room, porch, or garden) or if breakfast could be delivered to your room. This is something that needs to be discussed when the reservations are made.

Et Cetera

Q: Are guests ever served breakfast in bed at a B&B?

A: This service is usually limited to honeymooners, even though I once received it (as a non-honeymooner) at a B&B. If you are visiting an inn where breakfast in bed is offered and you wish to take advantage of this service, please be wearing something when breakfast is delivered. Simply being draped, with a top sheet, is insufficient.

Inn Tale: It was not a Kodak moment when an innkeeper delivered breakfast to newlyweds on their first morning as husband and wife. Awaiting their delivery of breakfast, they were propped in bed, au naturel, under the covers. When the husband (a rather prosperous gent around the middle) leaned forward to accept the breakfast tray, the bed collapsed and food flew everywhere. Not knowing what to do, the innkeepers also took flight, leaving the couple nude with their food.

Q: When staying in a cottage (separate from the main B&B inn, but a part of it) where breakfast is provided, is a guest expected to wash and put away the dishes used?

A: Sometimes instructions are posted letting guests know what the innkeepers expect concerning clean-up. Whenever I am staying at a B&B cottage, where I prepare my own breakfast with stocked items (cereal, toast, coffee cake, yogurt, fruit, coffee), I usually wash the dishes and put them away. However, as long as the dishes are rinsed and stacked, I think that is sufficient. It is not acceptable to leave dirty dishes sitting out or scattered about the place. Whenever there is a coffee pot in my room, I always rinse out the pot and toss out the coffee filter with the used grinds.

Q: Is there an online bulletin board where I can exchange information with other inngoers about B&Bs?

A: B&B-specific bulletin boards can be found at: www.bedandbreakfast.com Communities.aspx, www.innsite.com/rtbb, www.bandb.about.com (click "Forums" at top of page. Two other sites that have a bulletin board, for travelers to exchange information, are: independenttraveler.com (click "Boards" at top of page) and http://boards.travelocity.com.

Online bulletin boards, newsgroups, and forums provide an excellent way for travelers to exchange information. The last time my husband and I went to England, we needed accommodations close to Gatwick. Of course, I wanted to stay at a B&B. I posted a notice, outlining what we desired, on a British Travel Forum. Within 30 minutes, I had the information I needed. The B&B was delightful, though modest by American standards, and the innkeeper even provided "pick up/delivery service" to/from the airport. Use the bulletin boards for receiving and sharing information, but please do not use them as a way to "trash" inns or innkeepers. If you have an unpleasant experience at an inn, you can relate this without going into damaging (or even libelous) details.

Q: I love candles and incense and often travel with my own. Is it acceptable to burn candles at an inn?

A: Always ask for permission before burning candles. Incense is best left at home. It travels through an inn's heating/air-conditioning system, and its aroma is not appreciated by everyone. Open flames often violate an inn's insurance coverage.

Be aware that "blackening" the wicks of candles is the proper way of displaying them. It does not provide license for burning the candles.

Q: If I am flying in, is it appropriate to ask the innkeeper to pick me up from the airport?

A: Not unless they promote a pick-up service, which only a few do. Otherwise, rent a car or hail a taxi.

Q: Should I call the innkeeper by his or her first name?

A: That is the preference of most innkeepers, and they will probably call you by your first name (unless you indicate otherwise).

Q: What if there are bugs in my room?

A: All inns use a pest control service, but some of these rascals are impossible to get rid of entirely--like the infamous Palmetto water bug (euphemism for roach) that likes to creep around the Lowcountry. Ladybugs love B&Bs and seem to converge upon them.

One innkeeper framed a poem she wrote about how much ladybugs adore her inn.

Inn note: At one of the most elegant inns I have experienced, a roach jumped onto my pillow just as I was getting ready to lie down upon it. Another time, I found a dead "water bug" floating in a top-rated inn's toilet--one that even had the "seal-of-cleanliness" paper strap across it. *Bugs happen.*

Q: I enjoy picking up memorabilia from inns I visit. Do inns ever offer, for sale, special items reminiscent of their inn?

A: Definitely. Small corner or "cupboard" gift shops are frequently found in inns, and they often offer a wide variety of items with the inn's name or logo. Items include mugs, terry cloth robes, artwork, cookbooks, Christmas ornaments, magnets, and a host of other things to remind you of your stay at the inn.

My home study is dotted with mementos from visits to inns and special mementos given to me by innkeeper friends.

Q: **What if I have an accident while at a B&B (soiled sheets, become ill, etc.)?**

A: Even though accidents are embarrassing, the innkeeper (or housekeeper, if there is one) needs to be notified as soon as possible. Accidents happen, and it is better for the innkeeper to hear about it from you—especially if it involves breakage or a stain that needs immediate attention to keep from becoming permanent. If the damage is significant, then offering to pay for its repair or replacement is the least you can do.

Q: Is it acceptable to ask an innkeeper to do my personal laundry or to request permission to use the inn's laundry facilities?

A: I suspect most innkeepers would be thrilled to do your laundry *if* you would not mind taking some of theirs home to do in return. But, unless you are willing to do that, then you need to do your *own* laundry (or pay to have it done by someone who is in the laundering business—innkeepers are not). Neither is it appropriate to ask for permission to use an inn's laundry facilities. However, if you are a long-termer at the inn, the innkeeper may offer the use of the laundry facilities to you. If so, provide your own supplies.

There is a distinct difference between service and servitude. An innkeeper's charge is to provide the former, not the latter.

Q: What is considered a "suite" at a B&B?

A: I define a "suite" the same way the dictionary does: "a series of self-contained, connected rooms used as a living unit." However, I have found the term used loosely in the lodging industry, including B&B inns. Even if a room is large enough to be five rooms, yet it is just one open room, I consider it a "large room"--not a suite. Spacious rooms, including a sitting area and/or a kitchenette, are often promoted by inns as "suites." However, unless the rooms are separated by dividing walls, I do not categorize it as a suite.

If you are unable to differentiate between rooms and suite online, contact the innkeeper and inquire about the specifics.

Q: Is it okay to take food into my room at an inn?

A: Avoid taking in "fast food" or pizza into inn rooms. Doing so can result in stains, an offensive lingering smell (which can float into other rooms), and result in problems with rodents and/or ants. However, if a snack is provided at the inn, innkeepers usually do not object to you carrying it to your room. Just make sure not to put wet-bottomed glasses onto stainable wooden furniture or marble tops. Always use coasters, when provided.

Q: Is it okay to take some of the inn's hangers with me if I need extra ones?

A: No problem. Just mail them back when you get home--just in case the next guest needs an extra one. It shouldn't be any more trouble for you to mail hangers back to the inn than for the innkeeper to go purchase replacements for the ones you take.

If staying at an inn straps you financially to the point that you will not be able to afford to purchase your next roll of toilet paper, then, perhaps, you should consider more budget-oriented accommodations.. Inns are not paper product providers. Rule of thumb: never tuck anything into your suitcase or garment bag that you would be embarrassed for the innkeeper to discover if an "inspection check" were being made. Most guests are totally trustworthy.

Q: What should I do if I leave something at the inn? Will the innkeeper be willing to mail it to me?

A: Most inns have a "lost and found" box. Just call and let the innkeeper know what you left and the area (if you know). Chances are, you are more likely to have it returned than if you had left it at a motel or hotel. However, it is the responsibility of the guest to pay for the postage and handling of a returned item.

If you should inadvertently take the inn's keys home with you, the innkeepers would appreciate your thoughtfulness in mailing them back to the inn as soon as possible.

Q: Is it okay to make suggestions, face-to-face to an innkeeper, on how I feel their inn could be improved?

A: Most innkeepers are appreciative of helpful suggestions. Just remember, an innkeeper's inn is their "baby," and sometimes suggestions are not wanted or appreciated.

Unless I am specifically asked for recommendations by an innkeeper, I usually do not offer them. When grievances are voiced, always express them to the innkeeper privately. PAII (Professional Association Innkeepers International) often reminds innkeepers: "A complaint is a Gift" which is also the title of a book addressing this issue.

Q: Are the guest books found in the bedrooms of many B&Bs for compliments, suggestions, or both?

A: Most innkeepers hope guests will record something positive about their visit in the guestbook. Suggestion cards are often left out for appraisals and comments.

These books are not intended for writing odes of love to your beloved or anything of an offensive nature to others.

Q: Is it okay to take home a book from an inn's library that I have not completed reading or a video that I would like to view?

A: Even with the best of intentions, things "promised to be returned" often are not. Some inns offer a "book swap" program so guests may take a book in exchange for leaving one behind. However, it is best not to put an innkeeper on the spot by asking for the special favor of taking home a book or video. Magazines found in guest rooms, except for the local freebies, are to be left in the room for future guests.

Q: When I would like to express gratitude, in a special way, to an innkeeper for extra kindnesses extended me during my visit, how can I do this?

A: Just a hand-written thank-you note, expressing your gratitude, is always appreciated and cherished by innkeepers. If the inn has a special theme or the innkeeper is a collector of a specific item, send a surprise gift that can be displayed in the inn to remind the innkeepers of how their efforts are appreciated.

Q: What if an innkeeper presents me with a gift? Do I need to reciprocate in a like manner?

A: The most gracious way to reciprocate is with a heart-felt "thank you." Some people are natural "givers" and enjoy sharing with others. They are not seeking anything in return.

When a gift is given out of generosity, gratitude, or for no reason at all, accept it in the manner in which it is intended--and recycle the kindness to someone else when an opportunity arises. It always does.

B&Bs are Endless in their Uniqueness

Ashley River Bed & Berth
Charleston, SC

Pictures of Inns
of Advisory Board Members

Adams Edgeworth Inn
Monteagle, TN
www.assemblyinn.com

Bufflehead Cove Inn
Kennebunkport, ME
www.buffleheadcove.com

Casa Sedona
Sedona, AZ
www.casasedona.com

Chalet Club
Chimney Rock, NC
www.chaletclub.com

Folly Castle
Petersburg, VA
www.follycastle.com

Four Rooster Inn
Tabor City, NC
www.4roosterinn.com

Granite Steps
Savannah, GA
www.granitesteps.com

Harmony House
Catawba, SC
www.harmonyhousebb.com

Hayne House
Charleston, SC
www.haynehouse.com

The Hope and Glory Inn
Irvington, VA
www.hopeandglory.com

Iron Mountain Inn
Butler, TN
www.ironmountaininn.com

John Penrose Virden House
Lewes, DE
www.virdenhouse.com

The Nicholson House
Athens, GA
www.nicholsonhouseinn.com

Prestwould B&B
Flat Top, WV
www.prestwould.com

Red Horse Inn
Landrum, SC
www.theredhorseinn.com

St. Francis Inn
St. Augustine, FL
www.stfrancisinn.com

Basic Table Manners

The understanding and application of good table manners makes a statement about one's background and experience. Some regions and individuals are more manners-conscious than others, and cultural differences must also be considered—especially when traveling abroad.

Whether having a country-style breakfast at a casual B&B, a lavish morning repast at an historic inn, or a sumptuous dinner at an upscale restaurant, good manners are important. Knowing which utensil to use when, as well as other basics, enables one to avoid being uneasy or self-conscious during mealtime. However, the most important "table rule" is mealtime pleasantness and consideration of those with whom the meal is being shared.

A brief overview of dining etiquette is bulleted below. Excellent Web sites are available providing detailed information on dining and social etiquette. Suggested links are listed on page 129. A reliable etiquette book (such as *Emily Post's Advice for Every Dining Occasion* by Elizabeth L. Post) is a must for every home library.

- After being seated at the table, place the napkin in your lap. After the meal is over, leave your napkin placed loosely next to your plate. It should neither be crumpled nor left on the chair.

- A correctly set table has utensils arranged in the order they are to be used—from the outside to the inside. For example, the outer fork is the first fork used (usually for a salad or an appetizer). This same rule applies to the spoons and knives (located on the right side of the plate). Glasses are placed to the right of the plate since the majority of folks are right-handed.

- Food is served from the left side, and plates are removed from the right side. Likewise, when passing food at the table, it is served to the right (received from one's left).

- When someone requests that the salt be passed, it is passed along with the pepper. While en route to the person making the request, it is not to be used by others.

- Straw-sipping is fine at fast-food restaurants, but straws are only to be used for stirring at nicer establishments.

- Unless you are adept at using chopsticks, only use one utensil at a time (except when cutting, simultaneously, with a fork and knife). The empty hand is placed in the lap, *not* on the table.

- Once a utensil has been used, it must never touch the table again.

- A spoon is the utensil-of-choice for most fruit-type dishes (often the first breakfast course at inns).

- After eating food served in a compote or bowl, placed upon a plate, the spoon is placed on the plate (not left in the fruit or dessert dish).

Table Taboos

- Talking while food is in the mouth
- Talking on cell phones
- Blowing on hot foods or beverages
- Sopping bread into gravy or sauces
- Smoking
- Nose-blowing

- Picking teeth or using a toothpick
- Slurping soup
- Plate or bowl clanging (trying to scoop up last bites or drops)
- Putting elbows on the table or feet in the chair

Et Cetera

• Beepers and cell phones should be silenced during meal time at a restaurant or an inn. Many restaurants now request this courtesy.

• Even though requesting a take-home bag has become common place and acceptable at most restaurants (except for the most exclusive), this is not an appropriate request at an inn.

• In consideration of other paying guests, crying or misbehaving children need to be removed from a public dining area.

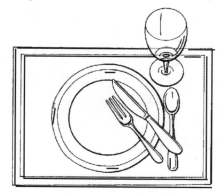

When finished eating, place your knife and fork in the position shown above. This signals that your plate is ready to be removed from the table.

Related Web Links

www.westernsilver.com/etiquette.html
www.cuisinenet.com/glossary/tableman.html
www.unlv.edu/Tourism/etiquette.html
www.visatablelinen.com
www.ryangrpinc.com/table_demo.html

If you have an etiquette-related question, you may send it to:
etiquette@emilypost.com

These Lowcountry oaks were once just two little "nuts,"
but they "held their ground" and survived the fury of Hurricane Hugo

Meet the Authors

Our Story

Mother and Daughter-- Partners and Friends

Malyssa and Maxine Pinson
Mother's Day 2001

It is not who or what we were yesterday that matters.
It is who and what we are today,
and the hope of who and what we may become tomorrow.

From Feisty Foes
to Forever Friends

by Maxine Pinson

*E*leven years ago it would have been disastrous for my twelve-year-old daughter, Melissa, and me to have been left alone in a dangerous place like a kitchen. No doubt about it, one of us would have whopped the other one over the head with a frying pan within a matter of moments. The only uncertainty was who would get the first blow and who would win that day's battle.

If Melissa and I had to travel together, I sat behind the wheel up-front, and she sat in the mini-van's way-back yonder spot. The tension between the two of us was so caustic that we would not even sleep in the same room if we had to travel together. I would pay extra just to have a wall between us. Whenever I was home with Melissa alone at night, I slept with my bedroom door locked and a motion detector on. She did not have to worry about me going up to her room. It was such a disaster, I would not allow the exterminator to go into the sty for two years. Melissa and Myra, her guinea pig, lived like two little rats in a room that was knee-high with impossible-to-decipher stuff.

Six years ago, when Melissa was sixteen-years-old, I no longer had to worry about what would happen if we were left alone or daily battles. Melissa had become a teenage runaway. For two-and-a-half unbearable years, we had no clue where she was. There were times when we did not know if our daughter was dead or alive. Both possibilities were real, and each was haunting. Meanwhile, my husband, Bill, and I were facing another crisis. Our twenty-one year old daughter, Celia, was dying of a rare form of non-Hodgkin's lymphoma—mycosis fungoides. There were many days, during this time, when I was convinced I had died and gone to Hell. When I realized I was still roaming planet Earth, I decided Hell would probably be like a five-diamond resort in comparison. There were times when I wanted to die, prayed to die, asked others to pray for me to die. It was just that bad. I had neither the desire nor the energy for living a life that had become so painful.

More than anything in my life-to-date, Malyssa represents, to me, the manifestation of hope fulfillment and answered prayer. I am grateful that the many prayers (by me and so many others) for Malyssa's safe return and restoration were answered; I am thankful the prayers (prayed to a merciful God of love and grace) for my demise were unanswered.

Today I cannot imagine life without Malyssa, and I look forward to our time together. Seldom does a day pass that we do not see each other, chat by phone, or correspond by e-mail. Without Malyssa's support, encouragement, sensitivity, intelligence, sense-of-humor, keen eye-for-detail, affirmations, and confidence in my ability, *Lowcountry Delights* simply would not be. I love you, 'lyssa!

In 1999, shortly before her twentieth birthday, Melissa decided to change the spelling of her name to *Malyssa*. I sensed her desire to adopt a new spelling of her name was a statement of the "new" person she had become. I understood the message I felt my daughter was trying to convey, and I respected her decision to do so. The road Malyssa traveled was a difficult one, but I feel it has made her a stronger and more compassionate human being. She has become a woman I am proud to call "daughter" and "friend."

Malyssa and I worked, diligently, on *Lowcountry Delights* for nine months. During these busy months, Malyssa and I spent much time together (usually with Barrister and/or Chymarra napping nearby) collecting recipes, testing recipes, typing recipes, editing recipes, *screaming* at recipes. After being involved in publishing for almost twenty-five years, I understood the basics. However, compiling a cookbook/travel guide, as inclusive as *Lowcountry Delights*, entailed far more than I anticipated. By the time we went to press, I felt like a baby had been delivered. And, yes, all of our "labor pains" were negated by the overwhelming excitement of what we had jointly accomplished and the enthusiasm from others.

As we spent time working together on *Lowcountry Delights,* there were times when each of us inevitably did things annoying to the other. Yet, not once was a cross word or look exchanged, not even when we were working under a tight deadline and totally exhausted. Our relationship was tested in swirling waters and survived. Not only did our relationship survive, it flourished and became strengthened through our valuing of each other's gifts and goals.

In spite of the long hours and frustrations involved, neither of us would trade our experience of creating *Lowcountry Delights* for anything. Not all of our work was difficult, by any means. Our visits to delightful Lowcountry inns and restaurants provided the extra fuel we needed to keep on keeping on; the memories created, while on these trips, provided refueling when we needed rejuvenating.

Traveling together, one of us would drive while the other did cookbook work on one of our laptops. Unlike ten years ago, we both sat up front. We even enjoyed listening to the same music—well, most of the time. No more staying in separate rooms; in fact, we sometimes shared the same bed. During and after dinner each evening, we relaxed and enjoyed each other's company. Whether sitting in a back corner of an earthy-type eatery or on the upper veranda of an antebellum plantation home, we spent time sharing, laughing and talking about things of importance in our lives. During these times, I feel we learned a lot from each other, and we became closer than I ever thought possible.

So, what's the next chapter in our story? The completion of *52 Scrolls*. Malyssa's name will appear first on this book, because she is the one who conceived and initiated it. Her part is already complete; she is now sitting in the editor's chair reminding me of my deadline. The story behind *52 Scrolls* is one difficult to hear while remaining dry-eyed. I respect and appreciate Malyssa's courage and willingness to share her part of our story with others. Each of us hopes our experience will provide encouragement and hope for other daughters and mothers going through difficult times.

As far as we know, there is no book comparable to *52 Scrolls* in style or content. It is slated for release in 2005. Until then, Malyssa and I will continue making up for the years we lost by savoring every moment of the time we have together now.

"The present is a *gift*, and that is why it is called a *present*." This saying may appear trite, but it is full of truth.

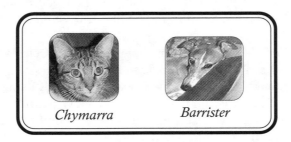

Chymarra   *Barrister*

Learning to Cook

by Malyssa Pinson

*T*wo years ago, it would have been nearly impossible for me to do any real cooking in my closet-sized kitchen. I lived in a studio apartment where everything was designed to fit into a small space. There is nothing wrong with that—I did not mind pulling down my Murphy-style bed (from its storage spot in the wall) each night. It did not bother me that I never had to tell company which door lead to the bathroom—it was the only door, other than the entrance to the apartment. However, the kitchen was almost non-functional and provided little incentive for trying to cook anything.

The mini-fridge, wedged into my kitchenette, had a small compartment that someone named a "freezer." The tiny cubicle was not large enough to even store an individual-sized pizza. The burners on the stove were so close together that I didn't think two of them could be used safely at the same time. When I did cook something simple, like a bag of rice or brownies out of a box, the entire apartment filled up with so much smoke I longed for more than one window in the place to provide ventilation.

All of this, along with the fact that I did not have much experience cooking in the first place, made me a pretty unlikely candidate for co-authoring a cookbook. I thought my mother had lost her mind, for sure this time, when she first told me about her cookbook idea. Yet, in spite of some of her crazy-sounding ideas, Mom has an uncanny knack for sticking with them and making them work. Her track record leaves little room for me to think, "That's not such a great idea!" I've learned to trust her on these things and see what happens.

This particular thing, producing the first copy of our cookbook/travel guide, happened pretty fast. Since my kitchen was so small, all the testing for the first edition of *Lowcountry Delights* was done in the kitchen of my parents' home. It was there, with my mother, that I learned most of what I now know about cooking. In fact, we *both* learned a lot by testing the recipes contributed by different inns and restaurants in the area—ones we personally experienced, enjoyed, and selected.

When my mother's "idea" developed into a joint success for both of us, I found myself the co-author of a real cookbook! Not only had I learned how to cook, but before long, I had a kitchen I could enjoy cooking in. That's right, I left the studio apartment for a bigger place with a real kitchen and lots of windows!

Eight months later, when it was time to start working on our book's revised edition, I was able to do some of the recipe testing, on my own, at home. The first recipe I tried was one for pecan pie. Mom thought it would be a good one for me to start with since it is one of the cookbook's easier recipes. I just needed to pick up a few things at the store—Karo syrup, pecans, sugar—and I would be all set. I already had eggs. Well, actually, they were Egg Beaters I had in my freezer. Before leaving for the store, I placed the "eggs" on the kitchen counter to thaw.

I knew Karo syrup was a corn syrup, so I assumed it would be shelved with corn oil, vegetable oil, and other cooking oils. I was wrong. Instead, it was sitting on a shelf with Aunt Jemima's maple syrup and other pancake toppings. I searched down quite a few aisles before I figured out that one. But, I knew I'd have no problem finding the next item on my list: pecans. Obviously, they would be with the almonds, peanuts, macadamia nuts, and other kinds of nuts. When I got home, much to my annoyance, I discovered I had bought salted and roasted pecans—the type used for snacking. I did not think that was the flavor I wanted to create in my Southern pecan pie! At that point, I decided to call it a night and bake the pie the next day.

The next morning, after returning from the grocery store with the right pecans, I realized the Egg Beaters were still sitting on the kitchen counter from the day before. I felt absolutely ridiculous. I realized if I returned to the grocery store a third time, it would almost be like making a separate trip for each ingredient called for in the pie. I was just *not* going to do that. So, I used the well-thawed "eggs" I already had. Later, when I removed the pie from the oven, it was an evenly-colored charcoal black; I knew it was not going to make any difference if the eggs used were good or not. I would not be serving that pie to anyone—not even my parents' dog

Hey, I never claimed to be a gourmet cook! But since "charcoaling" my pecan pie, I have tested lots of recipes in my new kitchen that have been edible. Not only have they been edible, but they have also been delicious. Right after the first edition of our cookbook came out, I invited my parents over for dinner on Father's Day and impressed them with an especially complicated-looking recipe (Filet Mignon with Potatoes Napolean and Apple Bacon Spinach, page 37). The recipe calls for two things I had never used before: a mandoline (used to cut potatoes into waffle-style chips) and a grill. I side-stepped using a mandoline, which I didn't have, by substituting frozen "waffle-fries." I learned how to use my hand-me-down grill as I prepared the steaks on it. After assembling the filets, spinach, and waffled potato-fries, I was so pleased with the attractive presentation that I almost didn't want it to be eaten. But it was eaten, every single bit of it. I thought maybe I could pass for a gourmet cook after all!

Now it is almost time to send the revised edition of *Lowcountry Delights* to press. Not only can I now find my way around the grocery store, but I feel much more comfortable in the kitchen—and it isn't just because I have enough space to turn around without bumping into something. With such wonderful restaurants around, like the ones we have selected for this book, I can understand why cooking at home is becoming a dying art. But, I, for one, hope it survives. I promise that most of these recipes can easily be prepared at home, even by a novice cook. I know first-hand.

The first edition of *Lowcountry Delights*, our first book and venture as partners, will always spark special memories for my mother and me. My first-try pecan pie, the first recipe I tested for the second edition of our cookbook, does not provoke such a positive memory! Yet, just like my first-try pecan pie was a learning experience for me, the first edition of our cookbook/travel guide proved to be a significant learning experience for both of us. Now as we go to press with the revised edition, I feel our second edition of *Lowcountry Delights* is comparable to the filet mignon I served so proudly. I think you will see why!

**Malyssa prepares another dinner for her dad, on his birthday,
using a recipe from *Lowcountry Delights***

52 SCROLLS

The story of how two head-strong women,
Mother and Daughter,
Rebuild their shattered relationship
In a special way.

Malyssa Pinson
Maxine Pinson

The heart-wrenching and tumultuous journey

which follows the spontaneous combustion of a mother undergoing a "mid-life crisis"

as her younger daughter struggles with the crises of a troubled adolescence—

and the poignant experiences re-uniting them

into a close, loving, and accepting relationship cherished by each.

A must-read for any parent needing hope and encouragement
during years of teen-age turbulence

Slated for 2006
scrolls52@aol.com

The Lowcountry

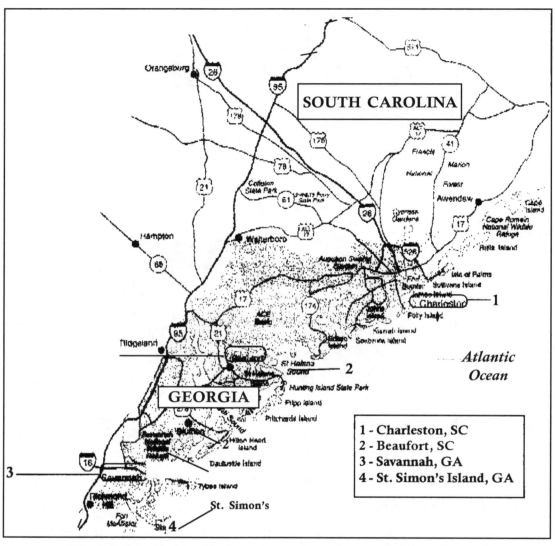

1 - Charleston, SC
2 - Beaufort, SC
3 - Savannah, GA
4 - St. Simon's Island, GA

The lay-of-the-land in The Lowcountry (sometimes spelled Low Country)
is defined by its name. It is flat land, barely above sea level. It is also a region
impassioned with a sense-of-place which embodies a spirit as high as the land is low.

Mileage between Cities

Charleston to Awendaw: 26 miles
Charleston to Beaufort: 69 miles
Charleston to Moncks Corner: 37 miles
Charleston to Mt. Pleasant: 6 miles
Charleston to Savannah: 108 miles
Charleston to Summerville: 23 miles
Charleston to St. Simon's: 185 miles

Savannah to Beaufort: 41 miles
Savannah to Charleston: 108 miles
Savannah to Moncks Corner: 119 miles
Savannah to St. Simon's: 86 miles
Savannah to Summerville: 101 miles
Savannah to Tybee Island: 17 miles
Beaufort to St. Simon's: 123 miles

Index & Order Forms

Index of Recipes

Eggs/Frittatas/Omelets/ Quiches/Soufflés/Stratas

French Toast/Blintzes/ Pancakes/Waffles

Fruit

Main Dish Casseroles and One-Dish Meals

We hope you enjoy our book!

Maxine   Malyssa

Malyssa and Maxine Pinson at one of their first
book signings during the summer of 2002.

Notes

INNside Scoop

"Everything You Ever Wanted to Know About Bed & Breakfast Inns"
plus
Inntertaining Inn Tales

by
Maxine Pinson
Introduction by Sandra W. Soule

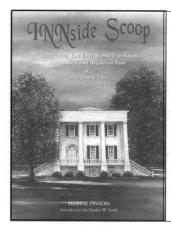

Order book toll-free:
1-800-871-8977
or online at:
www.innmarketing.com/orderform.htm
(an order form is also on page 222)

***

$14.95 + S&H

✔ *Over 80 photos of B&Bs (through-out US) plus listing of their Web sites*

✔ *Over 275 inn-related questions addressed with innformative and inntertaining answers*

✔ *Over 60 true illustrative "Inn Tales"— amusing, incredible, touching, outrageous*

✔ *Helpful information for inngoers, first-timers as well as the seasoned inngoer*

✔ *Table of Contents and Listing of Questions addressed in book may be seen online at:* **www.innsidescoop.com/is.htm**

✔ *A perfect gift for people who enjoy staying at bed and breakfast inns, or ones interested in checking them out!*

Published by
B&B and Country Inn Marketplace
927 Lenoir Rhyne Blvd., SE--Hickory, NC 28602
www.innmarketing.com
innsales@charter.net
1-800-871-8977

"Here is one of the industry's leading advocates delivering another publication to delight and entice innkeepers and inngoers alike. With her years of B&B/inn travel and her inimitable wit and perception, Maxine delivers an unmistakable love for the art of innkeeping while 'telling it like it is'."

— Jerry Phillips (Past Executive Director, PAII)

Order Form for

INNside Scoop

(Read more about book on page 223)

Please send me _____ copies of *INNside Scoop* @ *$14.95* each   _____

Shipping & Handling: Add *$4.95* per book   _____

NC residents add 7% sales tax   _____

TOTAL   _____

VALUE PACK

Purchase 4 books for *$44.85*   _____

Shipping & Handling *$10.00*
(sent to 1 address)   _____

NC residents add 7% sales tax   _____

TOTAL   _____

Reseller Prices Available

Call **1-800-871-8971**
or e-mail:
innsidescoop@innmarketing.com
for an order form and details.

Fill out form and Fax to: **828-328-8243**

Mail to: **The B&B and Country Inn MarketPlace**
926 Lenoir-Rhyne Blvd., SE
Hickory, NC 28602

Payment Method

Make checks payable to: The B&B and Country Inn Marketplace

Charge to: M/C or VISA (circle which) _____ Exp. _____

Cardholder's Name _____   Signature _____

Ship To:

Name _____

Address _____

City _____ State _____ Zip _____

Telephone _____ E-mail _____

_____ *I would like book autographed to:*

_____

Order Form for
Lowcountry Delights Cookbook & Travel Guide--2nd Edition
by Maxine & Malyssa Pinson

"Featuring Recipes from Favorite Lowcountry Inns & Restaurants"
(in Savannah & St. Simon's Island, GA--Beaufort & Charleston, SC)

www.thefoodscoop.com/lcd.html (links to a printable order form)

Please send me _____ copies of *Lowcountry Delights* @ $19.95 each _____

Shipping & Handling: Add $4.95 per book _____

GA residents add 6% sales tax _____

TOTAL _____

VALUE PACK

Purchase **4** books for *$72.00* _____

Shipping & Handling *$10.00*
(sent to 1 address) _____

GA residents add 6% sales tax _____

TOTAL _____

_____ **I would like this book autographed to:**

_____

Fill Out Form below and Send By Mail or Fax:

Send payment (check or a charge order) to:
SSD, Inc.
22 W. Bryan Street--PMB 202
Savannah, GA 31401
(Make check payable to SSD, Inc.)

Fax order form
(for charge orders only)
912~232~8550
E-mail inquiries to:
LCdelights@cs.com

Charge to: M/C or VISA (circle which) _____ Exp. _____

Cardholder's Name _____ Signature _____

Ship To:

Name _____

Address _____

City _____ State _____ Zip _____

Telephone _____ E-mail _____